William Gilham

Gilham's School of the Soldier and School of the Company

For Infantry and Rifle Drill

William Gilham

Gilham's School of the Soldier and School of the Company
For Infantry and Rifle Drill

ISBN/EAN: 9783337136789

Printed in Europe, USA, Canada, Australia, Japan

Cover: Foto ©ninafisch / pixelio.de

More available books at **www.hansebooks.com**

GILHAM'S

i

SCHOOL OF THE SOLDIER

AND

SCHOOL OF THE COMPANY,

FOR

INFANTRY AND RIFLE DRILL.

———•———

AUGUSTA, GEORGIA:
BRYAN & THOMPSON, PUBLISHERS

SCHOOL OF THE SOLDIER.

GENERAL RULES.

1. The object of this school is the individual instruction of the soldier; it should be taught with the greatest possible care and precision, as on it depends the efficiency of the instruction of the company, which is again, so necessary to that of the battalion, and from that of the battalion to the evolutions of the line, where an entire army is manœuvred with as much precision as a single company.

The instructor should never require a movement to be executed until he has fully explained it, and joined example to precept by performing the movement in person. He should accustom the soldier to take for himself the position required, correcting him when necessary, and should labor to prevent the formation of a habit of carelessness in the execution of the movements.

Each movement should be thoroughly understood before passing to another. After they have been properly executed in the order laid down, the instructor should no longer confine himself to that order. The men should be allowed to rest for a few moments, frequently, in the earlier stages of their instructions and as often at other times as the instructor may think necessary to prevent weariness, which is the prelude to carelessness. When they are at attention, however, he should not allow any looking to the right or left; no changing to position, or laughing, or whispering, etc., so common among volunteers and militia. Here is the place to make the individual soldier, to give him habits of attention, teach him subordination, etc. If he does not acquire them in this school, it will be too late when he is advanced in the company.

At the command rest, the soldier is no longer required to preserve immobility, or to remain in his place. If the instructor wishes merely to relieve the attention of the soldier, he commands, *in place*—rest; the soldier is then only required to keep one of his feet in place; if he wishes to move that foot, the other is first brought up to its proper position.

The *school of the soldier* is divided into three parts, the first comprehending what ought to be taught to recruits without arms; the second, the manual of arms, the loadings and firings; the third the principles of alignment, the march by the front, the different steps, the march by the flank, the principles of wheeling, and those of change of direction. In this school, the company is broken up into small squads, the number of men in each squad being proportioned to the number of instructors; the squad for the first and second part should be as small as possible, and the men placed in single rank; for instruction in the third part, two or more squads of about equal proficiency should be united.

PART FIRST.

In this part, the men should be without arms, and about one pace apart.

Position of the Soldier.

2. Heels on the same line, as near each other as the conformation of the men will permit; because, if one were in the rear of the other, the shoulder on that side would be thrown back.

The feet turned out equally, and forming with each other something less than a right angle; because, if one foot were turned out more than the other, a shoulder would be deranged, and if both feet be too much turned out, it would not be practicable to give the body its proper position.

4 — MANUAL FOR VOLUNTEERS AND MILITIA.

The knees straight, without stiffness; because, if stiffened, constraint and fatigue would be unavoidable.

The body erect on the hips, inclining a little forward, because it gives stability to the position. Soldiers are at first disposed to project the belly and throw back the shoulders when they wish to hold themselves erect, from which result many inconveniences in marching; it is, therefore, important that the instructor should be particular to enforce this rule at the beginning.

The shoulder square, and falling equally; if the shoulders are advanced beyond the line of the breast, and the back arched, (the defect called *round-shouldered*,) the man cannot align himself, nor use his piece with skill. In correcting this defect, the instructor will take care that the shoulders are not thrown too much to the rear, causing the body to project, and the small of the back to curve.

The arms hanging naturally; elbows near the body; palms of the hands turned a little to the front, the little finger behind the seam of the pantaloons. These positions are important to the *shoulder-arms*, to prevent the man from occupying more space in ranks than is necessary, and to keep the shoulders in proper position.

The head erect, and square to the front, without constraint; the chin slightly drawn in; the eyes fixed straight to the front, in order to prevent derangement of the shoulders, and striking the ground at the distance of about fifteen paces.

3. The instructor having given the squad the position of the soldier without arms, will now teach the turning of the head and eyes. He will command

1. *Eyes*—RIGHT. 2. FRONT.

At the word *right*, the soldier will turn his head gently, so as to bring the inner corner of the left eye in a line with the buttons of the coat, the eyes fixed on the line of the eyes of the men in the same rank. At the command FRONT the head will resume the direct or habitual position. The instructor will take care that the movement of the head does not derange the squareness of the shoulders, and that the men do not acquire a habit of throwing down the head in dressing.

The movement of *Eyes*—LEFT will be executed by inverse means.

Facings.

4. Facing to the right and left will be executed in one *time*, or pause. The instructor commands:

1. *Squad.* 2. (*Right or left*)—FACE.

At the word FACE, raise the *right* foot slightly, turn on the *left* heel, to the right (or left), raising the left toe a little, and then replace the right heel beside the left, and on the same line. The face should always be through a right angle, and should be executed by the feet and legs; the body moving around to the right (or left) without twisting or constraint. The instructor should labor to keep the body steady, and to prevent the formation of the habit of bending the knees, or *springing*.

5. The full face to the rear is always to the *right*, and is executed in two *times*, or pauses. The instructor commands:

1. *Squad.* 2 ABOUT—FACE.

First motion. At the word *about*, the soldier will turn far enough on the left heel to bring the left toe directly to the front, at the same time carrying his left foot to the rear, the hollow opposite to, and full three inches from the left heel, the feet square to each other. The back of the right hand is placed a little above the right hip, and the body is turned to the right sufficiently to give ease to the position.

Second motion. At the word *face*, the soldier raises his toes a little, turns upon both heels, faces to the rear, keeping his legs straight, and draws back the right heel by the side of the left, at the same time dropping his right hand by his side.

Balance Step.

6. Before commencing the march the soldier should always be instructed in the balance step, the object of which is to teach him the free movement of his limbs, while at the same time preserves perfect squareness of the shoulders, with the greatest steadiness of the body; no labor should be spared to attain this object, which lies at the very foundation of good marching.

The squad being at attention, the instructor commands:

Left foot—FORWARD.

At this command the soldier will throw his left foot gently forward, about twenty-four inches, balancing his body well on the right foot without changing the position of the shoulders, and without the body losing its erect position. The toe should be turned out as in the position of the soldier; the foot about three inches from the ground and very nearly parallel to it, the toe being very slightly depressed.

At the command :

Left foot—REAR.

The left foot is brought gently back, the ball of the left foot close to the right heel, the leg straight, toe raised, and heel depressed,

As soon as the soldier becomes steady in the new position, the instructor repeats the command, *left foot forward*, then *left foot rear*, for several times, and then commands :

HALT,

at which the left foot, either advanced or to the rear, is brought to the right, as in the position of the soldier.

The instructor then causes the soldier to balance on the right foot, by advancing and retiring the right, as has been directed for the left.

The Direct Step.

7. After the soldier is sufficiently instructed in the balance step to execute it on either foot without losing his balance, the instructor will proceed to instruct him in the mechanism of the direct step.   For this purpose he will command :

1 By the numbers—Forward.   2. ONE.

At the command *one*, the soldier will throw forward the left foot as in the position of *left foot forward*, the instructor then commands :

Two.

At this command, the weight of the body is thrown forward, the left foot striking the ground without shock, at the distance of twenty-eight inches from the right ; the body assumes the perpendicular position, and the right foot is brought up to the position of *right foot rear*.

The right foot is then brought forward at the command *one*, and the step completed at the command *two* ; thus the squad is made to advance step by step.   The *halt* is executed as in the *balance step*.

8. When the squad is sufficiently instructed in the mechanism of the direct step, the instructor will cause it to take up the march in common time ; for this purpose he will command :

Squad forward—Common time   2. MARCH.

At the command *forward*, the soldier will throw the weight of his body on the right leg, without bending the left knee.

At the command *march*, he will smartly, but without a jerk, carry straight forward the left foot twenty-eight inches from the right, the sole near the ground, the leg extended, the toe a little depressed, and both it and the knee slightly turned out; he will at the same time throw the weight of the body forward, and plant flat the left foot, without shock, precisely at the distance where it finds itself from the right when the weight of the body is brought forward, the whole of which will now rest on the left foot.   The soldier will next in like manner, advance the right foot and and plant it as directed for the left, the heel twenty-eight inches from the heel of the left foot, and thus continue the march without crossing the legs, or striking one against the other, without turning the shoulders, and always preserving the face direct to the front. Common time is executed at the rate of ninety steps to the minute.

When the instructor wishes to arrest the march he commands:

1. Squad.   2. HALT.

The command <i>halt</i> should be given just as one foot has come to the ground, and the other is raised for making the next step ; the soldier instinctively completes the pace with the raised foot, and brings the other firmly to its place beside it. By careful attention to this rule a large command may be as readily halted at the same instant, as a single individual.

9. The principles of the step in quick time are the same as for common time ; it is executed, however, at the rate of 110 steps per minute. After the soldier is well established in the length and swiftness of the step at common time, he should be practised in quick time, as it is the pace best adapted to marches the manœuvres, etc.

The instructor wishing the squad to march in quick time, commands :

1 Squad forward.   2. MARCH.

Principles of the Double Quick Step.

10. The length of the double quick step is thirty-three inches, and its swiftness is at the rate of 165 steps per minute. This step is designed especially for light troops, such as light infantry and riflemen, and to them it is indispensible ; its utility has, however, been so frequently demonstrated of late years, as to make it proper that it should form a part of the instruction of all infantry troops.

The instructor wishing to teach his squad the principles and mechanism of the double quick step, commands :

1. Double quick step.   2. MARCH.

At the command <i>double quick step,</i> the soldier will raise his hands to a level with his hips, the hands closed, the nails towards the body, the elbows to the rear and well drawn in towards the body.

At the command <i>march,</i> he will raise his left knee as high as possible without derangement of the body, keeping his leg from the knees down in a vertical position, the toe depressed ; he will then replace his foot in its former position.

At the command <i>two,</i> he will execute with the right leg what has just been prescribed for the left, and the alternate movement of the legs at the commands <i>one, two,</i> will be continued until the command :

1. Squad   2. HALT.

At the command <i>halt,</i> the soldier will bring the foot which is raised by the side of the other, and at the same time dropping his hands by his side will resume the position of the soldier without arms.

When the squad has learned to execute the step properly, the instructor will repeat the words <i>one, two,</i> in more rapid succession, and will finally drop them, leaving the files to execute the step in their own time. The instructor will see that the step is taken in rapid succession, and that none of the files lose the step.

11. The soldier being sufficiently established in the principles of this step, the instructor will command :

1 Squad, forward   2. Double quick.   3. MARCH.

At the command <i>forward,</i> the soldier will throw the weight of his body on the right leg, without bending the left knee.

At the command <i>double quick,</i> he will place his arms as indicated above

At the command <i>march,</i> he will carry forward the left foot, and plant it, the toe first, at the distance of thirty-three inches from the right, the leg slightly bent, and the knee somewhat raised ; he will then execute with the right foot what has just been prescribed for the left. This alternate movement of the legs will take place by throwing the weight of the body on the foot that is planted, and by allowing a natural, oscillatory motion to the arms. The feet should not be raised too much, a common fault with beginners, and the body should incline slightly forward.

The double quick step may be executed with different degrees of swiftness. Under urgent circumstances, the cadence of this step may be increased to 180 per minute. At this rate a distance of 4000 yards would be passed over in about twenty-five minutes.

The men should also be exercised in running; the principles are the same as for the double quick step, the only difference consisting in a greater degree of swiftness.

It is reccommended in marching in double quick time, or the run, that the men should breathe as much as possible through the nose, keeping the mouth closed.

PART SECOND—OR MANUAL OF ARMS.

General Rules.

12. The instructor will not pass the soldiers to this second part until they are well established in the position of the body and in the manner of marching at the different steps.

In the manual of arms each command will be executed in one *time* (or pause), but this time will be divided into motions, the better to make known the mechanism, and to secure uniformity and precision in the movements.

The rate (or swiftness) of each motion, in the manual of arms, is fixed at the nineteenth part of a minute ; but the instructor will, at first, look more particularly to the execution of the motions, without requiring a nice observonce of the cadence, to which he will bring the men progressively, and after they have become a little familiarized with the use of the weapon.

The motions relative to the cartridge, to the rammer, and to the fixing and unfixing of the bayonet, cannot be executed at the rate prescribed : or even with uniform swiftness ; the instructor will, however, labor to have these motions executed with promptness and regulasity.

The last syllable of the command will decide the brisk execution of the first motion of each time (or pause). The commands *two*, *three*, and *four*, will decide the brisk execution of the other motions. As soon as the men comprehend well the positions of the several motions of a time, they will be taught to execute the time without resting on its motions ; the mechanism of the time must, however, be observed as well to give perfect use to the weapon, as to prevent carelessness or slighting of the motions. When the men have acquired sufficient proficiency to execute the times without resting, the instructor must be careful to have the proper cadence observed ; great promptness in the execution of the motions is not incompatible with the observance of a pause between them, so that they may be executed at the prescribed rate—that is, of ninety to the minute. Those instructors who insist most upon the strict observance of this rule, are those whose squads execute the manual in the best manner.

Principles of Shouldered Arms.

13. Each soldier being in *the position of the soldier*, the instructor will cause him to turn up the left hand without bending the wrist, the left fore-arm only acting. The instructor will raise the piece perpendicularly, and place it as follows :

The piece in the left hand, the arm very slightly bent, the elbow back near the body, the palm of the hand pressing on the outer flat of the butt ; the outer edge of the latter on the upper joints of the fingers, the heel of the butt between the middle and fore-fingers, the thumb on the front screw of the butt plate, the remaining fingers under the butt, the butt more or less kept back according to the conformation of the man, so that the piece, seen from the front, shall appear perpendicular, and, also, that the movement of the

MANUAL FOR VOLUNTEERS AND MILITIA.

thigh, in marching, may not raise it or cause it to waver; the stock, below the tail-band, resting against the hollow of the shoulder, just within the joint, the right arm hanging naturally.

Soldiers on first bearing arms are liable to derange their position, and particularly to distort the shoulders, which, causing the musket to lose its point of support, they drop the left hand to prevent the musket from falling from the shoulder, which again causes that shoulder to droop, a curvature of the side, spreading of the elbows, etc. The instructor will be careful to correct all these faults by continually rectifying the position; he will avoid fatiguing the men too much in the beginning, but labor to render this position so natural and easy by degrees, that they may remain in it a long time without fatigue.

The instructor will also take great care that the musket be not carried too high or too low; if too high, the left elbow would spread out, the soldier would occupy too much space in ranks, and the musket would be unsteady; if too low, the files would be too close, the man would not have the necessary space to handle his musket with facility, the left arm would become too much fatigued, the shoulder would droop, etc.

The manual of the musket will be taught in the following order: The instructor commands:

Support—ARMS.
One time and three motions.

14. *First motion.* With the right hand seize the small of the stock briskly, four inches below the lock, raising the piece a little, but not turning it.

Second motion. Take the left hand from the butt; extend the left fore-arm upward across the body and under the hammer, the left hand flat on the right breast.

Third motion. Drop the right arm smartly to its position. The squad being at *support arms*, the instructor commands:

Carry—ARMS.
One time and three motions.

15. *First motion.* Carry quickly the right hand to the small of the stock.

Second motion. Place the left hand under the butt, as in the position of shoulder arms.

Third motion. Let fall smartly the right hand to its position, and drop with the left, at the same time, the piece into the position of *shoulder arms,*

Present—ARMS.
One time and two motions.

16. *First motion.* Turn the piece with the left hand, the lock out, and seize the small of the stock at the same time with the right hand, the piece perpendicular and detached from the shoulder, the left hand remaining under the butt.

Second motion. Complete the turning inwards of the piece, so as to bring it erect before the centre of the body, the rammer to the front, the right hand under and against the guard: seize it smartly at the same time with the left hand just above the lock, the thumb extended along the barrel and on the stock, the left fore-arm resting on the body without constraint, and the hand at the height of the elbow.

Shoulder—ARMS.
One time and two motions.

17. *First motion.* Turn the piece with the right hand, the barrel to the front, raise and support it against the left shoulder with the right hand, drop the left under the butt, the right hand resting on, without grasping the small of the stock.

Second motion. Drop quickly the right hand into its position.

Order—ARMS.
One time and two motions.

18. *First motion* Drop the piece   , seize it at

the same time with the right hand, above and near the tail-band; quit the hold of the left hand, and carry the piere opposite to the right shoulder, the rammer to to the front, the little finger behind the barrel, the right hand supported against the hip, the butt three inches from the ground, the piece erect, the left hand hanging by the side.

Second motion. Let the piece slip through the right hand to the ground without shock, and take the position about to be described.

Position of Order Arms

19. The hand low, the barrel between the thumb and forefinger extended along the stock: the other fingers extended and joined; the muzzle about two inches from the right shoulder; the rammer in front; the toe of the butt against, and in a line with, the toe of the right foot, the barrel perpendicular.

20. When the instructor wishes to repose in this position, he commands:

REST.

At this command the soldier will not be required to preserve silence or steadiness. They, however, will not quit their rank without special permission.

21. When the instructor wishes the men to pass from this position to that of silence and steadiness, he commands:

1 *Attention.* 2. SQUAD.

At the second word, the men will reserve the position of *order arms*, and remain firm and silent.

Shoulder—ARMS.

One time and two Motions.

22. *First motion.* Raise smartly the piece with the right hand, carry it against the left shoulder, turning it, so as to bring the barrel to the front; at the same time place the left hand under the butt, and slip the right hand down to the lock.

Second motion. Let the right hand fall briskly to its position.

Charge—BAYONET.

One time and two Motions.

23. *First Motion.* Make a half face to the right on the left heel, bring the left toe directly to the front, at the same time place the right foot behind, and at right angles with the left, the hollow of the right foot opposite to, and about three inches from the left heel; turn the piece with the left hand, the lock outwards, and seize the small of the stock at the same time with the right hand, the musket perpendicular, and detached from the shoulder, the left hand under the butt.

Second motion. Bring down the piece with the right hand, letting it fall firmly into the left, the latter seizing it a little in advance of the tail band, the barrel up, the left elbow near the body, the right hand against the hip, the point of the bayonet as high as the eye.

Shoulder—ARMS.

One time and two Motions

24. *First motion.* Face to the front by turning on the left heel, bring up the right by the side of the left heel; at the same time bring up the piece with the right hand to the left shoulder, and place the left hand under the butt.

Second motion. Let the right hand fall promptly into position.

Load in ten times.

1. LOAD.

One time and two motions.

25. *First motion.* Drop the piece by a smart extension of the left arm, seize it

with the right hand above and near the lower band; at the same time carry the right foot forward, the heel against the hollow of the left foot.

Second motion. Drop the piece with the right hand along the left thigh, seize it with the left hand above the right, and with the left hand let it descend to the ground, without shock, the piece touching the left thigh, and the muzz e opposite the centre of the body; carry the right hand quickly to the cartridge box and open it.

2. *Handle*—CARTRIDGE.
One time and one motion.

26. Seize a cartridge with the thumb and the next two fingers, and place it between the teeth.

3. *Tear*—CARTRIDGE.
One time and one motion.

27. Tear the paper down to the powder, hold the cartridge upright between the thumb and two next fingers, near the top; in this position place it in front of and near the muzzle, the back of the hand to the front.

4. *Charge*—CARTRIDGE.

28. Fix the eye on the muzzle, turn quickly the back of right hand towards the body, in order to discharge the powder in the barrel, raise the elbow to the height of the wrist, shake the cartridge, force it into the muzzle, and leave the hand reversed, the fingers closed, but not clenched.

5. *Draw*—RAMMER.
One time and three motions.

29. *First motion.* Drop the right elbow smartly, and seize the rammer between the thumb and fore-finger bent, the other fingers shut; draw it smartly extending the arm, seize the rammer again at the middle between the thumb and fore-finger, the hand reversed, the palm to the front, the nails up, the eyes following the movement of the hand, clear the rammer from the pipes by again extending the arm.

Second motion. Turn rapidly the rammer between the bayonet and the face, closing the fingers, the rammers of the rear rank grazing the right shoulders of the men of the same file in front, the rammer parallel to the bayonet, the arm extended, the butt of the rammer opposite to the muzzle but not yet inserted, the eyes fixed on the muzzle.

Third motion. Insert the butt of the rammer, and force it down as low as the hand.

6. *Ram*—CARTRIDGE.
One time and one motion.

30. Extend the arm to its full length to seize the rammer between the right thumb extended and the fore-finger bent, the other fingers closed; with force ram home twice and seize the rammer at the small end between the thumb and fore-finger bent, the other fingers closed, the right elbow touching the body.

7. *Return*—RAMMER.
One time and three motions.

31. *First motion.* Draw the rammer briskly, re-seize it at the middle between the thumb and fore finger, the hand reversed, the palm to the front, the nails up, the eyes following the hand, clear the rammer from the barrel by extending the arm.

Second motion. Turn the rammer rapidly between the bayonet and the face, closing the fingers, the rammers of the rear rank grazing the right shoulders of the men in the same file in front, the rammer parallel to the bayonet, the arm extended, the little end of the rammer opposite to the first pipe, but not yet inserted, the eyes fixed on that pipe.

Third motion. Insert the small end, and with the thumb, which will follow the movement, force it as low as the middle band ; raise the hand quickly, a little bent, place the little finger on the butt of the rammer, and force it down ; lower the left hand on the barrel to the extent of the arm without depressing the shoulder.

8. *Cast*—ABOUT.

One time and two motions.

32. *First motion.* With the left hand bring up the piece vertically against the left shoulder, seize it smartly with the right hand at the small of the stock, and slide the left hand down as low as the chin.

Second motion. Make a half face to the right on the left heel, bring the left toe to the front, place the right foot at the same time close behind, and at right angles with the left, the hollow of the right foot against the left heel ; carry the piece opposite to the right shoulder ; bring down the piece with the right hand into the left, which will seize it at the tail band, the thumb extended on the stock, the butt under the right fore-arm, the small of the stock against the body, and about two inches under the right breast, the muzzle at · height of the eye, the left elbow supported against the side, the right hand grasping the small of the stock.

9. *Prime.*

One time and one motion.

33. Place the thumb of the right hand on the hammer (the fingers remaining under and against the guard), and half-cock the piece ; brush off the old cap, and with the thumb and first two fingers of the right hand take a cap from the pouch, place it firmly on the cone by pushing it down with the thumb, and seize the piece by the small of the stock.

10. *Shoulder*—ARMS.

One time and two motions.

34. *First motion.* Face to the front by turning on the left heel ; at the same time bring the piece briskly with the right hand to the left shoulder, and place the left hand under the butt.

Second motion. Let the right hand fall smartly into its position at *shoulder arms.*

READY. (From the position of *prime.*)

One time and one motion.

35. Place the thumb of the right hand on the hammer (the fingers remaining under and against the guard), cock the piece, and seize the small of the stock.

READY. (From the position of *shoulder arms.*)

One time and four motions.

36. *First motion.* Turn the piece with the left hand, the lock to the front seize it at the small of the stock with the right hand ; at the same time make a half face to the right on the left heel, bringing the left toe to the front, and placing the right foot behind, and at right angles to the left, the hollow of the foot against the left heel. ·

Second motion. Bring the piece with the right hand to the middle of the body, place the left hand just above the lock, the thumb extended along the stock at the height of the chin, the counter (or S) -plate turned towards the body, the rammer obliquely to the left and front.

Third motion. Place the thumb on the hammer, the fore-finger under and on the guard, the other three fingers joined to the first, the elbow at the height of the hand.

Fourth motion. Close the right elbow smartly to the body in cocking, without bending the wrist , seize the piece by the small of the stock, let it descend along the body in the left hand to the tailband, which will remain at the height of the shoulder.

AIM.

One time and one motion.

37. Raise the butt to the shoulder, the left elbow a little down, shut the left eye direct the right along the barrel, drop the head upon the butt to catch the object, and place the fore-finger on the trigger. The rear rank will at the same time, carry the right foot about eight inches towards the left heel of the man next on his right.

FIRE.

One time and one motion.

38. Apply the fore-finger with force to the trigger without further lowering or turning the head, and remain in that position.

LOAD. (From the Fire.)

One time and two motions.

39. *First motion.* Bring back the piece quickly with both hands, depress the butt strongly by extending the right arm, and carry it with the arm thus extended to the left side, the barrel to the front and opposite to the left shoulder the left hand at the height of the chin, the back of the hand to the front, the left forearm touching the stock; at the same time face to the front and carry the right foot forward, the heel against the hollow of the left foot.

Second motion. Let go the handle with the right hand, let the piece descend through the left to the ground, without shock, and take the position of the second motion of *load.*

*Shoulder—*ARMS. (From the *Fire.*)

One time and two motions.

40. *First motion.* Bring back the piece with both hands, face to the front, carry the piece against the left shoulder, and place the left hand under the butt.

Second motion. Let the right hand fall smartly to its position.

The squad being in the position of *aim,* the instructor, to habituate the soldiers to wait for the word *fire,* sometimes commands :

*Recover—*ARMS.

One time and one motion.

41. Withdraw the finger from the trigger, throw up the muzzle smartly, and retake the position of the fourth motion of *ready.*

The men being in this position, if the instructor wishes them to come to a shoulder, he commands :

*Shoulder—*ARMS.

42. At the word *shoulder,* the squad will face to the front, and bring their pieces to the middle of the body again; the left thumb at the height of the chin, the little finger just above the lock, next place the right thumb on the head of the hammer, support the fore-finger on the trigger, sustain the hammer carefully in its descent at the same time, to the position of half-cock, then seize the the small of the stock with the right hand. At the word *arms,* carry the piece to the shoulder smartly, and take the position of *shoulder arms.*

To load in four times (or pauses.)

43. The instructor commands :

1. *Load in four* TIMES. 2. LOAD.

Execute the first time of loading, handle cartridge, tear cartridge, charge cartridge.

TWO.

44. Draw rammer, enter it as far as the hand, and ram twice.

THREE.

46. Return rammer, cast about, and prime.

FOUR.

46. Execute the tenth time of loading.

47. The soldiers being at a shoulder, when the instructor may wish to return bayonets, he commands;

*Unfix—*BAYONETS.

One time and three motions.

First motion. Drop the piece by a smart extension of the left arm, seize it with the right hand above and near the tail band.

Second motion. Drop the piece with the right hand along the left thigh, seize it with the left hand above the right, lengthen out the left arm, rest the butt on the ground, without shock, and carry the right hand at the same time to the bayonet, with the thumb lower the clasp against the stop, and then seize the bayonet at the socket and shank.

Third motion. Wrest off the bayonet, return it to the scabbard, place the little finger on the butt of the rammer, lower the left hand along the barrel in extending the arm, without depressing the shoulder.

*Shoulder—*ARMS.

One time and three motions.

48. *First motion.* Raise the piece with the left hand along the left side, the hand at the height of the chin, the fore-arm touching the piece, the barrel to the front ; drop at the same time the right hand to seize the piece a little above the handle, the fore-finger touching the cock, and the thumb on the counter-plate,

Second motion. Raise the piece with the right hand, drop the left, and place it under the butt, bring back the right heel to the side of the left, and on the same line ; support the piece with the right hand against the shoulder, in the position prescribed for *shoulder arms*, the right hand resting on, without grasping, the piece.

Third motion. Let fall smartly the right hand into its position by the side of the thigh.

*Fix—*BAYONET.

49. *First and second motions.* As the first and second motions of *unfix bayonet*, except that at the end of the second motion, the right hand will go to seize the bayonet by the socket and shank, so that the lower (now upper) end of the socket shall extend about an inch above the heel of the palm.

Third motion. Draw the bayonet from the scabbard, carry and fix it on the muzzle, turning the clasp towards the body with the right thumb ; place the little finger on the head of the rammer, lower the left hand along the barrel, in extending the arm.

*Shoulder—*ARMS.

The same as from the *Unfix bayonet.*

*Secure—*ARMS.

One time and two motions.

50. *First motion.* Seize quickly the piece with the right hand, the thumb on the counter-plate, and the fore-finger against the cock ; detach the piece from the shoulder at the same instant, the barrel to the front, seize it at the tail-band with the left hand the thumb extended on the rammer, the piece erect, opposite to the shoulder, the left elbow on the piece.

Second motion. Reverse the piece, pass it under the left arm, the left hand remaining at the tail-band, the thumb on the rammer to prevent it from sliding out, the little finger resting against the hip, and the right hand falling at the same time into its position.

Shoulder—ARMS.

One time and two motions.

51. *First motion.* Raise the piece with the left hand, but not too suddenly, lest the rammer should fly out; seize the handle with the right hand to support it against the shoulder, quit the hold of the left hand, and place quickly this hand under the butt.

Second motion. Let fall smartly the right hand under its position ; drop at the same time the piece into the position of *shouldered arms.*

Trail—ARMS.

one time and two motions.

52. *First motion.* As the first motion of *order arms.*

Second motion. Incline a little the muzzle to the front, the butt to the rear, and about three inches from the ground, the right hand, supported at the hip, will sustain the piece so that the men of the rear rank may not touch with their bayonets the men in front of them.

Shoulder—ARMS.

53. At the command *shoulder,* raise the piece perpendicularly in the right hand ; at the command *arms,* execute what has been prescribed for the shoulder from the position of *order arms.*

To right shoulder shift—ARMS.

One time and one motion.

54. Turn the piece with the left hand, the lock to the front, seize it at the same time with the right hand at the handle, place it on the right shoulder, the left hand not quitting the butt, the lock-plate upwards, the muzzle up ; sustain the piece in this position by placing the right hand on the flat of the butt ; let fall the left hand by the side.

Shoulder—ARMS.

55. Raise the piece by extending the right arm, seize it with the left hand above the lock, carry it against the left shoulder, turning the barrel to the front, the right hand being at the handle, place the left hand under the butt, and let the right fall into its position.

Arms—AT WILL.

One time and one motion.

56. Carry the piece at pleasure on either shoulder, or with one or both hands, the muzzle always up.

Shoulder—ARMS

57. Retake smartly the position of *shoulder arms.*

Inspection of Arms.

58. The squad being at ordered arms, and having the bayonet in the scabbard, if the instructor wishes to cause an inspection of arms, he will command :

Inspection of—ARMS.

One time and three motions.

First motion. Face to the right once and a half on the left heel, carrying the right foot perpindicularly to the rear of the alignment, about six inches from, and at right angles with, the left foot; seize promptly the piece with the left hand a little above the middle band, incline the muzzle to the rear without displacing the heel of the butt, the rammer turned towards the body ; carry at the same time the right hand to the bayonet and seize it as has been prescribed, No. 49.

Second motion. Draw the bayonet from the scabbard, carry and fix it on the muzzle; seize next the rammer, draw it as has been explained in loading it twelve times, and let it glide to the bottom of the bore.

Third motion. Face promptly to the front, seize the piece with the right hand, and retake the position of ordered arms.

The instructor will then inspect in succession the piece of each man in passing along the front of the rank. Each, as the instructor reaches him, will raise smartly his piece with his right hand, seize it with the left between the tail-band and the feather-spring, the lock to the front, the left hand at the height of the chin, the piece opposite to the left eye; the instructor will take it with the right hand at the handle, and, after inspecting it, will return it to the soldier, who will receive it back with the right hand, and replace it in the position of ordered arms.

When the instructor shall have passed him, each soldier will retake the position prescribed at the command *inspection of arms*, and return the rammer ; after which he will face to the front.

If, instead of inspection of arms, it be the wish of the instructor only to cause bayonets to be fixed, he will command :

*Fix—*Bayonet.

Take the position indicated, No. 139, (first motion), fix bayonets as has been explained, and immediately face to the front.

Bayonets fixed, if it be the wish of the instructor, after firing, to ascertain whether the pieces have been discharged, he will command :

*Spring—*Rammers.

Put the rammer in the barrel, as has been explained above, and immediately face to the front.

The instructor, for the purpose stated, can take the rammer by the small end, and spring it in the barrel, or cause each man to make the rammer ring in the barrel.

Each man, after the instructor passes him, will return rammer, and face to the front.

*Arms—*Port.

One time and one motion.

59. Throw the piece diagonally across the body, the look to the front seize it smartly at the same instant with both hands, the right at the handle, the left at the tail-band, the two thumbs pointing towards the muzzle, the barrel sloping upwards and crossing opposite to the point of the left shoulder, the butt, proportionally lowered. The palm of the right hand will be above, and that of the left under the piece, the nails of both hands next to the body, to which the elbows will be closed.

*Shoulder—*Arms.

One time and two motions.

First motion. Bring the piece smartly to the left shoulder, placing the left hand under the butt;
Second motion. Drop the right hand smartly by the side

MANUAL OF ARMS FOR THE RIFLE.

Principles of Shouldered Arms.

60. The soldier standing in the position of the soldier, the instructor causes him to bend the right arm slightly, and places the piece in it, in the following manner : The piece in the right hand—the barrel nearly vertical and resting in the hollow of the shoulder—the guard to the front, the arm hanging nearly at its full length near the body ; the thumb and fore-finger embracing the guard, the remaining fingers closed together, and grasping the swell of the stock just under the cook, which rests on the little finger.

Support—ARMS.
One time and three motions.

61. *First motion.* Bring the piece, with the right hand, perpendicularly to the front and between the eyes, the barrel to the rear ; seize the piece with the left hand at the lower band, raise this hand as high as the chin, and seize the piece at the same time with the right hand four inches below the cock.

Second motion. Turn the piece with the right hand, the barrel to the front ; carry the piece to the left shoulder, and pass the forearm extended on the breast between the right hand and the cock ; support the cock against the left fore-arm, the left hand resting on the right breast.

Third motion. Drop the right hand by the side.

Shoulder—ARMS.
One time and three motions.

62. *First motion.* Grasp the piece with the right hand under and against the left fore-arm ; seize it with the left hand at the lower band, the thumb extended ; detach the piece slightly from the shoulder, the left fore arm along the stock.

Second motion. Carry the piece vertically to the right shoulder with both hands, the rammer to the front, change the position of the right hand so as to embrace the guard with the thumb and forefinger, slip the left hand to the height of the shoulder, the fingers extended and joined, the right arm nearly straight.

Third motion. Drop the left hand quickly by the side.

Present—ARMS.
One time and two motions.

63. *First motion.* With the right hand bring the piece erect before the centre of the body, the rammer to the front ; at the same time seize the piece with the left hand half-way between the guide sight and lower band, the thumb extended along the barrel and against the stock, the fore-arm horizontal and resting against the body, the hand as high as the elbow.

Second motion. Grasp the small of the stock with the right hand below and against the guard.

Shoulder—ARMS.
One time and two motions.

64. *First motion* Bring the piece to the right shoulder, at the same time change the position of the right hand so as to embrace the guard with the thumb and fore-finger, slip up the left hand to the height of the shoulder, the fingers extended and joined, the right arm nearly straight.

Second motion. Drop the left hand quickly by the side.

Order—ARMS.
One time and two motions.

65. *First motion.* Seize the piece briskly with the left hand near the upper band, and detach it slightly from the shoulder with the right hand ; loosen the grasp of the right hand, lower the piece with the left, re-seize the piece with the right hand above the lower band, the little finger in rear of the barrel, the butt about four inches from the ground, the right hand supported against the hip, drop the left hand by the side.

Second motion. Let the piece slip through the right hand to the ground by opening slightly the fingers, and take the position about to be described.

Position of Order Arms.

66. The hand low, the barrel between the thumb and fore-finger extended along the stock ; the other fingers extended and joined ; the muzzle about

two inches from the right shoulder; the rammer in front; the too (or beak) of the butt, against, and in a lino with, the too of the right foot, the barrel perpendicular.

Shoulder—ARMS.

One time and two motions.

67. *First motion.* Raise the piece vertically with the right hand to the height of the right breast, and opposite the shoulder, the elbow close to the body; seize the piece with the left hand below the right, and drop quickly the right hand to grasp the piece at the swell of the stock, the thumb and fore.finger embracing the guard; press the piece against the shoulder with the left hand, the right arm nearly straight.

Second motion. Drop the left hand quickly by the side.

Load in nine times.

1. LOAD*

One time and one motion.

68. Grasp the piece with the left hand as high as the right elbow, and bring it vertically opposite the middle of the body, shift the right hand to the upper band, place the butt between the feet, the barrel to the front; seize it with the left hand near the muzzle, which should be three inches from the body; carry the right hand to the cartridge box.

2. *Handle*—CARTRIDGE.

One time and one motion.

69. Seize the cartridge with the thumb and next two fingers, and place it between the teeth.

3. *Tear*—CARTRIDGE.

One time and one motion.

70. Tear the paper to the powder, hold the cartridge upright between the thumb and first two fingers, near the top; in this position place it in front of and near the muzzle—the back of the hand to the front.

4. *Charge*—CARTRIDGE.

One time and one motion.

71. Empty the powder into the barrel; disengage the ball from the paper with the right hand and the thumb and first two fingers of the left; insert it into the bore, the pointed end uppermost, and press it down with the right thumb; seize the head of the rammer with the thumb and fore-finger of the right hand, the other fingers closed, the elbows near the body.

5. *Draw*—RAMMER.

One time and three motions.

72. *First motion.* Half draw the rammer by extending the right arm; steady it in this position with the left thumb; grasp the rammer near the muzzle with the right hand, the little finger uppermost, the nails to the front, the thumb extending along the rammer.

Second motion. Clear the rammer from the pipes by again extending the arm; the rammer in the prolongation of the pipes.

Third motion. Turn the rammer, the little end of the rammer passing near the left shoulder; place the head of the rammer on the ball, the back of the hand to the front.

---

*Whenever the loadings and firings are to be executed, the instructor will cause the cartridge-boxes to be brought to the front.

6. *Ram*—CARTRIDGE.
One time and one motion.

73. Insert the rammer as far as the right, and steady it in this position with the thumb of the left hand; seize the rammer at the small end with the thumb and fore-finger of the right hand, the back of the hand to the front; press the ball home, the elbows near the body.

7. *Return*—RAMMER.
One time and three motions.

74. *First motion.* Draw the rammer half-way out, and steady it in this position with the left thumb; grasp it near the muzzle with the right hand, the little finger uppermost, the nails to the front, the thumb along the rammer; clear the rammer from the bore by extending the arm, the nails to the front, the rammer in the prolongation of the bore.

Second motion. Turn the rammer, the head of the rammer passing near the left shoulder, and insert it in the pipes until the right hand reaches the muzzle, the nails to the front.

Third motion. Force the rammer home by placing the little finger of the right hand on the head of the rammer: pass the left hand down the barrel to the extent of the arm, without depressing the shoulder.

8. PRIME.
One time and two motions.

75. *First motion.* With the left hand raise the piece till the hand is as high as the eye, grasp the small of the stock with the right hand; half face to the right; place, at the same time, the right foot behind and at right angles with the left; the hollow of the right foot against the left heel. Slip the left hand down to the lower band, the thumb along the stock, the left elbow against the body; bring the piece to the right side, the butt below the right fore-arm—the small of the stock against the body and two inches below the right breast, the barrel upwards, the muzzle on a level with the eye.

Second motion. Half cock with the thumb of the right hand, the fingers supported against the guard and the small of the stock—remove the old cap with one of the fingers of the right hand, and with the thumb and fore-finger of the same hand take a cap from the pouch, place it on the nipple and press it down with the thumb; seize the small of the stock with the right hand.

9. *Shoulder*—ARMS.
One time and two motions.

76. *First motion.* Bring the piece to the right shoulder, and support it there with the left hand, face to the front; bring the right heel to the side of and on a line with the left; grasp the piece with the right hand as indicated in the position of *shoulder arms.*

Second motion. Drop the left hand quickly by the side.

READY.
One time and three motions.

77. *First motion.* Raise the piece slightly with the right hand, making a half face to the right on the left heel; carry the right foot to the rear, and place it at right angles to the left, the hollow of it opposite to, and against the left heel; grasp the piece with the left hand at the lower band and detach it slightly from the shoulder.

Second motion. Bring down the piece with both hands, the barrel upwards the left thumb extended along the stock, the butt below the right fore-arm the small of the stock against the body and two inches below the right breast, the muzzle as high as the eye, the left elbow against the side; place at the same time the right thumb on the head of the cock, the other fingers under and against the guard.

Third motion. Cock, and seize the piece at the small of the stock without deranging the position of the butt.

AIM.

78. As in the manual for the musket.

FIRE.

79. As in the manual for the musket.

LOAD.

One time and one motion.

80. Bring down the piece with both hands, at the same time face to the front and take the position of *load.* Each rear rank man will bring his right foot by the side of the left

The men being in this position, the instructor will cause the loading to be continued by the commands and means prescibed No. 69, and following.

If after firing, the instructor should not wish the recruits to reload, he will command :

Shoulder—ARMS.

One time and one motion.

81. Throw up the piece briskly with the left hand and resume the position of *shoulder arms* , at the same time face to the front, turn on the left heel, and bring the right heel on a line with the left.

Recover—ARMS.

82. The same as in the manual for the musket.
83. The soldiers being in the position of the third motion of *ready,* if the instructor should wish to bring them to a shoulder, he will command :

Shoulder—ARMS.

One time and one motion.

At the command *shoulder,* place the thumb upon the cock, the fore-finger on the trigger. Half-cock, and seize the small of the stock with the right hand. At the command *arms,* bring up the piece briskly to the right shoulder, and retake the position of shoulder arms.

The recruits been at shoulder arms, when the instructor shall wish to fix bayonets, he will command :

Fix—BAYONET.

One time and three motions.

84. *First motion.* Grasp the piece with the left hand at the height of the shoulder, and detach it slightly from the shoulder with the right hand.

Second motion. Quit the piece with the right hand, lower it with the left hand, opposite the middle of the body, and place the butt between the feet without shock ; the rammer to the rear, the barrel vertical, the muzzle three inches from the body ; seize it with the right hand at the upper band, band carry the left hand reversed to the handle of the sabre-bayonet.

Third motion. Draw the sabre-bayonet from the scabbard and fix it on the extremity of the barrel ; seize the piece with the left hand, the arm extended, the right hand at the upper band.

Shoulder—ARMS.

One time and two motions

85. *First motion.* Raise the piece with the left hand and place it against the right shoulder, the rammer to the front ; seize the piece at the same time with the right hand at the swell of the stock, the thumb and fore finger embracing the guard, the right arm nearly extended.

Second motion. Drop briskly the left hand by the side.

Charge—BAYONET.

One time and two motions.

86. *First motion.* Raise the piece slightly with the right hand and make a half face to the right on the left heel ; place the hollow of the right foot opposite to, and three inches from the left heel, the feet square : seize the piece at the same time with the left hand a little above the lower band.

Second motion. Bring down the piece with both hands, the barrel uppermost, the left elbow against the body ; seize the small of the stock, at the same time, with the right hand, which will be supported against the hip; the point of the sabre-bayonet as high as the eye.

Shoulder—ARMS.

One time and two motions.

87. *First motion.* Throw up the piece briskly with the left hand in facing to the front, place it against the right shoulder, the rammer to the front ; turn the right hand so as to embrace the guard, slide the left hand to the height of the shoulder, the right hand nearly extended.

Second motion. Drop the left hand smartly by the side.

Trail—ARMS.

One time and two motions.

88. *First motion.* The same as the first motion of *order arms.*

Second motion. Incline the muzzle slightly to the front, the butt to the rear and about four inches from the ground. The right hand supported at the hip, will so hold the piece that the rear rank men may not touch with their bayonets the men in the front rank.

Shoulder—ARMS.

89. At the command *shoulder,* raise the piece perpendicularly in the right hand, the little finger in rear of the barrel ; at the command *arms,* execute what has been prescribed for the *shoulder* from the position of *order arms.*

Unfix—BAYONET.

One time and three motions.

90. *First and second motions.* The same as the first and second motions of *fix bayonet,* except that, at the end of the second command. the thumb of the right hand will be placed on the spring of the sabre bayonet, and the left hand will embrace the handle of the sabre-bayonet and the barrel, the thumb extended along the blade.

Third motion. Press the thumb of the right hand on the spring, wrest off the sabre-bayonet, turn it to the right, the edge to the front, lower the guard until it touches the right hand, which will seize the back and the edge of the blade between the thumb and first two fingers, the other fingers holding the piece ; change the position of the hand without quitting the handle, return the sabre-bayonet to the scabbard, and seize the piece with the left hand, the arm extended.

Shoulder—ARMS.

One time and two motions.

91. *First motion.* The same as the first motion from *fix bayonet,* No. 85.

Second motion. The same as the second motion from *fix bayonet.*

Secure—ARMS.

One time and three motions

92. *First motion.* The same as the first motion of *support arms,* except with the right hand seize the piece at the small of the stock.

Second motion. Turn the piece with both hands, the barrel to the front ; bring it opposite the left shoulder, the butt against the hip, the left hand at the lower band, the thumb as high as the chin and extended on the rammer; the piece erect and detached from the shoulder, the left fore-arm against the piece.

Third motion. Reverse the piece, pass it under the left arm, the left hand remaining at the lower hand, the thumb on the rammer to prevent it from sliding out, the little finger resting against the hip, the right hand falling at the same time by the side.

Shoulder—Arms.
One time and three motions.

93. *First motion.* Raise the piece with the left hand, and seize it with the right hand at the small of the stock. The piece erect and detached from shoulder, the butt against the hip, the left fore-arm along the piece.

Second motion. The same as the second motion of *shoulder arms from a support.*

Third motion The same as the third motion of *shoulder arms from a support.*

Right shoulder shift—Arms.
One time and two motions.

94. *First motion.* Detach the piece perpendicularly from the shoulder with the right hand, and seize it with the left between the lower hand and guide light, raise the piece, the left hand at the height of the shoulder and four inches from it; place, at the same time, the right hand on the butt, the heak between the first two fingers, the other two fingers under the butt plate.

Second motion. Quit the piece with the left hand, raise and place the piece on the right shoulder with the right hand, the lock plate upwards: let fall, at the same time the left hand by the side.

Shoulder—Arms.
One time and two motions.

95. *First motion.* Raise the piece perpendicularly by extending the right arm to its full length, the rammer to the front, at the same time seize the piece with the left hand between the lower hand and guide-sight.

Second motion. Quit the butt with the right hand, which will immediately embrace the guard, lower the piece to the position of shoulder arms, slide up the left hand to the height of the shoulder, the fingers extended and closed. Drop the left hand by the side.

The men being at support arms, the instructor will sometimes cause pieces to be brought to the right shoulder. To this effect, he will command:

Right shoulder shift—Arms.
One time and two motions.

96. *First motion.* Seize the piece with the right hand, below and near the left fore-arm, place the left hand under the butt, the heel of the butt between the first two fingers.

Second motion. Turn the piece with the left hand, the lock plate upwards, carry it to the right shoulder, the left hand still holding the butt, the muzzle elevated; hold the piece in this position and place the right hand upon the butt, and let fall the hand by the side.

Support—Arms.
One time and two motions.

97. *First motion* The same as the first motion of *shoulder arms.*

Second motion Turn the piece with both hands, the barrel to the front, carry it opposite the left shoulder, slip the right hand to the small of the stock, place the left fore-arm extended on the breast, and let fall the right hand by the side.

Arms—At will.
One time and one motion.

98. At this command carry the piece at pleasure on either shoulder, with one or both hands, the muzzle elevated.

*Shoulder—*ARMS.

One time and one motion.

99. At this command, retake quickly the position of shoulder arms.

Inspection of arms.

100. The soldiers being at *ordered arms,* and having the sabre-bayonet in the scabbard, if the instructor wishes to cause an inspection of arms, he will command :

*Inspection—*ARMS.

One time and two motions.

101. *First motion.* Seize the piece with the left hand below and near the upper band, carry it with both hands opposite the middle of the body, the butt between the feet, the rammer to the rear, the barrel vertical, the muzzle about three inches from the body ; carry the left hand reversed to the sabre bayonet, draw it from the scabbard and fix it on the barrel; grasp the piece with the left hand below and near the upper band, seize the rammer with the thumb and fore-finger of the right hand bent, the other fingers closed.

Second motion. Draw the rammer as has been explained in *loading,* and let it glide to the bottom of the bore, replace the piece with the left hand opposite the right shoulder, and retake the position of *ordered arms.*

The instructor will then inspect the piece of each man, in passing along the front of the rank. Each, as the instructor reaches him, will raise smartly his piece with his right hand, seize it with the left between the lower band and guide sight, the lock to the front, the left hand at the height of the chin, the piece opposite the left eye, the instructor will take it with the right hand at the handle, and, after inspecting it, will return it to the man, who will receive it back with the right hand, and replace it in the position of *ordered arms.*

When the instructor shall have passed him, each soldier will retake the position prescribed at the command *inspection arms,* return the rammer, and resume the position of *ordered arms*

If, instead of *inspection of arms,* the instructor should merely wish to cause bayonets to be fixed, he will command :

*Fix—*BAYONET.

102. Take the position indicated No. 101, fix bayonets as has been explained, and immediately resume the position of *ordered arms.*

If it be the wish of the instructor, after firing, to ascertain whether the pieces have been discharged, he will command :

Spring RAMMERS.

This is done as in the manual for the musket.

To load in four times.

103. The first time will be executed at the end of the command ; the three others at the commands, two, three, and four.

The instructor will command :

1. *Load in four times.* 2. LOAD.

104. Execute the times to include charge cartridge.

TWO.

105. Exec; ute the times to include ram cartridge.

THREE.

106. Execute the times to include prime.

SCHOOL OF THE SOLDIER.

FOUR.

107. Execute the time of *shoulder arms.*

To load at will.

108. The instructor will next teach loading at will, which will be executed as loading in four times, but continued. and without resting on either of the times. He will command.

I. *Load at will* 2. LOAD.

The instructor will habitate the soldiers by degrees, to load with the greatest possible promptitude, each without regulating himself by his neighbor, and above all without waiting for him.

Firings.

109. The firings are direct or oblique, and will be executed as follows :

The direct fire.

The instructor will give the following commands :

1.*Fire by squad.* 2. *Squad.* 3. READY. 4. AIM. 5. FIRE. 6. LOAD.

The several commands will be executed as has been prescribed in the *Manual of Arms.* At the third command, the men will come to the position of *ready* as heretofore explained. At the fourth they will aim according to the rank in which each may find himself placed, the rear rank men inclining forward a little the upper part of the body, in order that pieces may reach as much beyond the front rank as possible.

At the sixth command, they will load their pieces, and return immediately to the position of *ready.*

The instructor will recommence the firing by the commands :

1. *Squad.* 2. AIM. 3. FIRE, 4. LOAD.

When the instructor wishes the firing to cease, he will command :

Cease firing.

At this command, the men will cease firing, but will load their pieces if unloaded, and afterwards bring them to a shoulder.

Oblique Firings.

110. The oblique firings will be executed to the right and left, and by the same commands as the direct fire, with this single difference, the command aim will always be proceeded by the caution, *right or left oblique.*

Position of two ranks in the Oblique Fire to the right.

At the command ready, the two ranks will execute what has been prescribed for the direct fire.

At the cautionary command, *right oblique,* the two ranks will throw back the right shoulder and look steadily at the object to be hit.

At the command aim, each front rank man will aim to the right without deranging the feet ; each rear rank man will advance the left foot about eight inches towards the right heel of the man next on the right of his file leader and aim to the right, inclining the upper part of the body forward and bending a little the left knee.

Position of the two ranks in the Oblique Fire to the left.

At the cautionary command, *left oblique,* the two ranks will throw back the left shoulder and look steadily at the object to be hit.

At the command *aim,* each front rank man will aim to the right without deranging the feet ; each rear rank man will advance the left foot about eight inches towards the right heel of the man next on the right of his file leader, and aim to to the left, inclining the upper part of the body forward and bending a little the right knee.

In both cases, at the command *load,* the men of each rank will come to the position of load as prescribed in the direct fire; the rear rank men bringing back the foot which is to the right and front by the side of the other. Each man will continue to load as if isolated.

To Fire by File.

111. The fire by file will be executed by the two ranks, the files of which will fire successively, and without regulating on each other, except for the first fire.

The instructor will command :

1. *Fire by File.* 2. *Squad.* 3. READY. 4. COMMENCE FIRING.

At the third command, the two ranks will take the position prescribed in the direct fire.

At the fourth command, the file on the right will aim and fire; the rear man in aiming will take the position indicated No. 118.

The men of this file will load their pieces briskly and fire a second time; reload and fire again, and so on in continuation.

The second file will aim, at the instant the first brings down pieces to reload, and will conform in all respects to that which has just been prescribed for the the first file.

After the first fire, the front and rear rank men will not be required to fire at the same time

Each man, after loading, will return to the position of ready and continue the fire.

When the instructor wishes the fire to cease, he will command :

Cease—FIRING.

At this command, the men will cease firing. If they have fired they will load their pieces and bring them to a shoulder ; if at the position of *ready*, they will half-cock and shoulder arms. If in the position of *aim*, they will bring down their pieces, half-cock and shoulder arms.

To fire by rank.

112. The fire by the rank will be executed by each entire rank, alternately. The instructor will command :

1. *Fire by rank.* 2. *Squad.* 3. READY. 4. *Rear Rank.* 5. AIM. 6 FIRE. 7. LOAD.

At the third command, the two ranks will take the position of *ready*, as prescribed in the direct fire.

At the seventh command, the rear rank will execute that which has been prescribed in the direct fire, and afterwards take the position of *ready*.

As soon as the instructor sees several men of the rear rank in the position of ready, he will command :

1. *Front Rank.* 2. AIM. 3. FIRE. 4. LOAD.

At these commands, the men in the front rank will execute what has been prescribed for the rear rank, but they will not step off with the right foot.

The instructor will recommence the firing by the rear rank, and will thus continue to alternate from rank to rank, until he shall wish the firing to cease, when he will command, *cease firing*, which will be executed as heretofore prescribed.

To fire and load Kneeling.

113. In this exercise the squad will be supposed loaded and drawn up in one rank. The instruction will be given to each man individually, without times or motions, and in the following manner.

The instructor will command :

FIRE AND LOAD KNEELING.

At this command, the man on the right of the squad will move forward

three paces and halt; then carry the right foot to the rear and to the right
of the left heel, and in a position convenient for placing the right knee upon
the ground in bending the left leg ; place the right knee upon the ground ;
lower the piece, the left fore-arm supported upon the thigh on the same side
the right hand on the small of the stock, the butt resting on the right thigh,
the left hand supporting piece near the lower band.

He will next move the right leg to the left around the knee supported on
the ground, until this leg is nearly perpendicular to the direction of the
left foot, and thus seat himself comfortably on the right heel.

. Raise the piece with the right hand and support tt with the left, holding it
near the lower band, the left elbow resting on the left thigh near the
knee ; seize the hammer with the thumb, the fore-finger under the guard,
cook and seize the piece at the small of the stock; bring the piece to the
shoulder, *aim* and *fire*.

Bring the piece down as soon as it is fired, and support it with the left
hand, the butt resting against the right thigh ; carry the piece to the rear
rising on the knee, the barrel downwards, the butt resting on the ground;
in this position support the piece with the left hand at the upper band,
draw cartridge with the right and load the piece, ramming the ball, if necessary, with both hands.

When loaded bring the piece to the front with the left hand, which holds
it at the upper band ; seize it at the same time with the right hand at the
small of the stock : turn the piece, the barrel uppermost and nearly horizontal, the left elbow resting on the left thigh ; half-cock, remove the old
cap and prime, rise, and return to the ranks.

The second man will then be taught what has just been prescribed for the
first, and so on through the remainder of the squad.

To fire and load Lying.

114. In this exercise the squad will be in one rank and loaded ; the instruction will be given individually and without times or motions.

The instructor will command :

FIRE AND LOAD LYING.

At this command, the man on the right of the squad will move forward
three paces and halt ; he will then bring his piece to an order, drop on both
knees, and place himself on the ground flat on his belly. In this position
he will support the piece nearly horizontal with the left hand, holding it
near the lower band, the butt end of the piece and the left elbow resting on
the ground, the barrel uppermost ; cock the piece with the right hand, and
carry this hand to the small of the stock ; raise the piece with both hands,
press the butt against the shoulder, and resting on both elbows, *aim* and
fire.

As soon as he as has fired, bring the piece down and turn upon his left
side, still resting on his left elbow ; bring back the piece until the cock is
opposite his breast, the butt end resting on the ground ; take out a cartridge
with right hand ; seize the small of the stock with this hand, holding the cartridge with the thumb and two first fingers ; he will then throw himself on his
back still holding the piece with both hands ; carry the piece to the rear,
place the butt between the heels, the barrel up, the muzzle elevated. In
this position, charge cartridge, draw rammer, ram cartridge, and return
rammer.

When finished loading, the man will turn again upon his left side, remove
the old cap and prime, then raise the piece vertically, raise, turn about, and
resume his position in the ranks.

The second man will be taught what has just been prescribed for the first,
and so on throughout the squad.

Bayonet Exercise.

115. The bayonet exercise in this book will be confined to two movements

the *guard against infantry* and the *guard against cavalry*. The men will be placed in one rank, with two paces interval, and being at shoulder arms, the instructor will command.

1. *Guard against Infantry.* 2. GUARD.
One time and two motions.

First motion. Make a half face to the right, turning on both heels, the feet square to each other ; at the same time raise the piece slightly, and seize it with the left hand above and near the lower band.

Second motion. Carry the right foot twenty inches perpendicularly to the rear, the right heel on the prolongation of the left, the knees slightly bent, the weight of the body resting equally on both legs ; lower the piece with both hands, the barrel uppermost, the left elbow against the body seize the piece at the same time with the right hand at the small of the stock, the arms falling naturally, the point of the bayonet slightly elavated.

*Shoulder—*ARMS.
One time and one motion.

Throw up the piece with the left hand, and place it against the right shoulder, at the same time bring the right heel by the side of the left and face to the front.

1. *Guard against Cavalry.* 2. GUARD.
One time and two motions.

Both motions the same as for *guard against infantry*, except that the right hand will be supported against the hip, and the bayonet held at the height of the eye, as in charge bayonet.

*Shoulder—*ARMS.
One time and one motion.

Spring up the piece with left hand and place it against the right shoulder, at the same time bring the right heel by the side of the left, and face to the front.

MANUAL OF THE SWORD OR SABRE, FOR OFFICERS.

POSITION OF THE SWORD OR SABRE, UNDER ARMS.

116. *The carry.* The grip in the right hand, which will be supported against the right hip, the back of the blade against the right shoulder.

TO SALUTE WITH THE SWORD OR SABRE.

Three times or pauses.

1. At the distance of six paces from the person to be saluted, raise the sword or sabre perpendicularly, the point up, the flat of the blade opposite to the right eye, the guard at the height of the shoulder, the elbow supported on the body.

2. Drop the point of the sword or sabre by extending the arm, so that the right hand may be brought to the side of the right thigh, and remain in that position until the person to whom the salute is rendered shall be passed, or shall have passed, six paces.

3. Raise the sword or sabre smartly, and resume the position first prescribed.

COLOR SALUTE.

117. In the ranks, the color-bearer, whether at a halt or in march, will carry the heel of the color-lance supported at the hip, the right hand generally placed on the lance at the height of the shoulder, to hold it steady. When the color has to render honors, the color bearer will salute as follows.

At the distance of six paces slip the right hand along to the height of the lance; lower the lance by straightening the arm to its fullest extent, the heel of the lance remaining at the hip, and bring back the lance to the habitual position when the person saluted shall be passed, or shall have passed, six paces.

PART THIRD.

118. When the men are well established in *the principles and mechanism of the step, the position of the body, and the manual of arms,* the instructor will unite from eight to twelve in a squad, in order to teach them the principles of alignment, the touch of the elbow in marching to the front, the principles of the march by the flank, wheeling from a halt, wheeling in marching, and the change of direction to the side of the guide. He will place the squad in one rank elbow to elbow, and number the men from right to left.

Alignments.

119. The instructor will at first teach the soldiers to align themselves man man, in order to make them understand the principles of alignment better; for this purpose, he will command the two men on the right flank to march two paces to the front, and having aligned (or *dressed*) them, he will cause the remainder of the squad to move up, as may successively called, each by his number, as *three, four,* etc., and align (or *dress*) themselves successively on the line of the first two men.

Each man, as designated by his number, will turn his head and eyes to right, as directed for *eyes right* in the first part, and march *two paces forward in quick time*, shortening the last step, so as to find himself about six inches behind the new line, which he ought never to cross; he will then move up steadily by the steps of two or three inches, the legs straight, to the side of the next man to him on the line, so that, without throwing the head or the shoulders out of place, he may find himself in the exact line with the files on his right, and touching elbows with the nearest one without opening out his arms.

The instructor seeing the line properly dressed, commands:

FRONT.

At which the men will turn their eyes to the front, and remain firm.

Alignments to the left will be conducted on the same principles.

120 When the men shall have learned to dress correctly man by man, without deranging the head or shoulders, and without jostling, the instructor will cause the entire squad to dress at once by the command:

Squad right (or left)—DRESS.

At this the squad, except the two men placed in advance as a basis of alignment, will move up in *quick time*, and place themselves on the new line according to the principles just laid down.

The instructor will superintend the dressing, and when he sees the greater number of the squad in their proper places, will command:

FRONT.

The instructor may afterwards order *this or that* file *forward* or *back*, designating each man by his number (or name). The file or files designated, will slightly turn the head towards the *right* (or *left*), to judge how much they ought to move up or back, place themselves on the line by moving an inch or two at a time, and then turn eyes to the front, without waiting for any command from the instructor.

121. Alignments to the rear will be executed on the same principles, the men stepping back a little beyond the line, and then dressing up according to the principles laid down in No. 119; the commands of the instructor are:

Right (or left) backwards DRESS.

To march to the front,

122. The squad being correctly aligned, and the instructor wishing to

march it to the front, he will place a well-instructed man on the right or left, according to the side on which he wishes the guide to be, and commands

1. *Squad forward.* 2. *Guide right (or left.* 3. MARCH.

At the command *march*, the squad will step off smartly with the left foot, and will take up *quick time*, unless otherwise specially ordered. *This rule is general.* The guide will take care to march straight to the front, keeping his shoulders always square with that line. The men will touch elbows lightly on the side towards the guide, maintaining the shoulders square to the front, no matter on which side the guide may be ; they should be careful not to open out the left elbow, or the right arm ; that they yeild to pressure coming from the side of the guide, and resist that coming from the side opposite ; that they recover by insensible degrees the touch of the elbow, if lost ; and if any files are before or behind the line, that they correct themselves by shortening or lengthening the step by almost insensible degrees. It is all important that the closet attention should be paid to each one of the above directions, otherwise the men cannot attain proficiency, and when they are advanced to the company drill, it will be impossible to secure promptness or accuracy in the manœuvres.

123. The men being established in the principles of the direct march, the instructor will exercise them in marching obliquely. The squad being in march, the instructor commands :

1. *Right (or left) oblique.* 2. MARCH.

At the command *march*, each man will make a half face to the right (or left), and will then march straight forward in the new direction. As the men no longer touch elbows, they will glance along the nearest files, towards the side to which they are obliquing, and will regulate their steps so that the right (or left) shoulder shall always behind the left (or right) shoulder of their next neighbor on the right (or left), and that his head shall conceal the heads of the other men on the right (or left). The men should be careful to preserve the same length of pace, and the same degree of obliquity. The guides must always be on the flank towards which the oblique takes place.

The instructor wishing to resume the direct march, will command :

1. *Forward.* 2. MARCH.

At the command *march*, each man will make a half face to the left (or right), and all will march straight fo the front, conforming to the principles laid down for marching to the front.

To march to the front in double quick time.

124. Instruction in the principles oft his step is recommended for all infantry troops ; it *may* be omitted for *infantry of the line*, but in no other case ; nothing but the imperative necessity for giving all of the time at the disposal of the instructor to instruction in the principles of the quick step and to the manœuvres, should prevent even infantry of the line from being thoroughly instructed in the principles of this step.

The squad being at a march in quick time, the instructor commands :

Double quick. 2. MARCH.

At the command *march*, which will be given when either foot is coming to the ground, the squad will step off in double quick time. The men should be careful to follow the rules already laid down for the march in the double quick step, and to preserve the alignment.

When the instructor wishes the squad to resume the quick step, he will command :

1. *Quick time.* 2. MARCH.

At the command *march*, which should be given when either foot is coming to the ground, the squad will retake the step in quick time.

If the squad is at a halt, and the instructor wishes to march at the double quick step he commands :

1 *Squad forward.* 2. *Guide right* (or *left*). 3. *Double quick.* 4. MARCH

The squad being on the march in double quick time, the instructor will occasionally cause it to mark time ; the men will then mark double quick time without altering the cadence. He will also cause them to pass from the direct to the oblique march, and the reverse, conforming to what has been prescribed for the oblique march.

In marching at *double quick time*, the men will always carry their pieces on the *right shoulder,* or at a *trail. This rule is general.*

If the instructor wishes the pieces carried at a trail, he will give the command *trail arms,* before the command *double quick.* If, on the contrary, this command is not given, the men will shift their pieces to the right shoulder at the command *double quick.* In either case, at the command halt, the men will bring their pieces to the position of shouldered arms. This rule is general.

To face about in marching.

125. If the squad be marching in quick, or double quick time, and the instructor should wish to march in retreat he will command :

1. *Squad right about.* 2. MARCH.

At the command march, which should be given at the instant the *right foot touches the ground,* the soldier will complete the next pace with the left foot, then turning to the right about on both heels, will step off with the left foot.

To March by the flank.

The squad being at a halt, and correctly aligned, the instructor will command :

1. *Squad, right*—FACE. 2. *Forward.* 3. MARCH.

At the command *face,* the squad will face to the right ; the even numbered men, after falling to the right, will step quickly to the right side of the odd numbered men, the latter standing fast, so that when the movement is executed the men will be formed into files of two men abreast, or *doubled.*

At the command *march,* the squad will step off smartly with the left foot ; the files keeping their dress, and preserving their intervals.

The march by the left flank will be executed by the same commands, substituting the word *left* for *right,* and by inverse means: in this case, the even numbered men, after facing to the left, will stand fast, and the odd numbered will place themselves on their left.

When the instructor shall wish to halt the squad, marching by the flank, and to cause it to face to the front, he will command :

1. *Squad.* 2. HALT. 3. FRONT.

At the second command the rank will halt, and afterwards no man will stir, although he may have lost his distance. This prohibition is necessary, to habituate the men to a constant attention to their distances.

At the command *front,* each man will front by facing to the left, if marching by the right flank, and by a face to the right, if marching by the left flank. The rear rank men will move quickly into their places, so as to form the squad into one rank again.

126. The squad being on the march by the flank, the instructor will cause it to change direction by commanding :

1. *By file left* (or *right*). 2. MARCH.

At the command, *march* the first file will change direction to the left (or right) in describing a small arc of a circle, and will then march strait forward ; the two men of this file, in wheeling, will keep up the touch of the elbows, and the man on the side to which the wheel is made, will shorten the first three or four steps, Each file will come successively to the wheel on the same spot where that which preceded it wheeled.

The instructor will also cause the squad to face by the right or left flank in marching, and for this purpose will command :

1. *Squad by the right* (or *left*) *flank.* 2. MARCH.

At the command *march*, which will be given a little before either foot comes to the ground, the men will turn the body, plant the foot that is raised in the new direction, and step off with the other foot without altering the cadence of the step. When the squad faces to the front or rear in marching, the men who find themselves in *rear* step to the right or left so as to form a single rank, each man in his place as in the beginning ; this is called the *undoubling* of files.

If when the squad is marching to the front or rear, the instructor causes it to march by a flank, the files will *double ;* when the squad is on the march to the front, and is faced by the right flank, the *even* numbers will step up to the right of the *odd* ones, as in the first instance in facing from a halt ; when it is marched by the left flank, the *odd* numbers should double on the left of the *even*, if the squad is marching to the rear, when it is faced by the right flank they will double on the *even* as in the last case, but if faced by the left flank the even will double to the right of the *odd* as in the first case.

The instructor will sometimes march by a flank without doubling files ; for this purpose he commands :

*In one rank, right—*FACE.

In marching at the *double quick*, however, the files will always be doubled

General principles of wheelings.

127. Wheelings are of two kinds ; from a halt, or on *fixed* pivots, and on the march, or on a *movable* pivot.

In wheelings from a halt, the pivot-man only turns in his place, without advancing or receding. In the wheels in marching, the pivot-man takes steps of nine or eleven inches, according as the squad is marching in quick or double quick time, so as to clear the wheeling point, which is necessary in order that, in a column composed of sections, platoons, or companies, the distances between the different parts of it shall not be lost, as will be more fully explained in the school of the company.

The man on the wheeling flank will take a full pace of twenty-eight, or thirty-three inches, according to whether the time is quick or double quick.

Wheeling from a halt, or on a fixed pivot.

128. The squad being at a halt, the instructor will place a well-instructed man on the wheeling flank to conduct it, and command :

I. *By squad, right wheel.* 2. MARCH.

At the command march, the squad will step off with the left foot, turning the head at the same time a little to the left, the eyes on the line of the eyes of the men to their left ; the pivot-man will merely mark time, gradually' turning his body, in order to conform himself to the movements of the marching flank ; the man who conducts this flank will take steps of twenty-eight inches, and from the first step advance the left shoulder a little, cast his eyes from time to time along the rank, and feel constantly, but lightly, the elbow of the next man on his right, but never push him. The other man will feel lightly the elbow of the next man to his right, resist pressure coming from the left, and yield to any coming from the right : each man will conform himself to the march of the men on the left, shortening his step more and more as he is nearer the right, or pivot.

The instructor will make the squad wheel round the circle once or twice before halting, in order to cause the principles to be better understood, and he will be watchful that the centre does not break or get too far in advance

He will cause the wheel to the left to be executed on the same principles.

When the inctructor wishes io arrest the wheel, he commands :

1. *Squad.* 2. HALT.

At the second command the squad will halt, and no man stir. The instructor going to the left (or right, if the wheel has been to the left) flank, will place the two outer men of that flank in the direction he may wish to give to the squad, without, however displacing the pivot, who will conform the line of his shoulders to this direction. The instructor will take care to have between these two men and the pivot, only the space neeessary to contain the other men. He will then command :

Left (or *right*)—DRESS.

At this the squad will place itself on the alignment of the men fixed as the bases, in conformity with the principles laid down for the alignments. As soon as the men are aligned, the instructor commands :

FRONT.

Wheeling in marching, or on a moveable pivot.

129. When the men have been brought to execute the wheel from a halt properly, they will be taught the wheel in marching.

For this end, the squad being on the march, when the instructor shall wish to cause it to change direction to the flank opposite the guide, he will command.

1. *Right* (or *left*) *wheel.* 2. MARCH.

The first command will be given when the squad is *four* paces from the wheeling point.

At the command march the wheel will be executed in the same manner as from a halt, except that the touch of the elbow will remain towards the *left* or marching flank, instead of the side of the actual pivot ; that the pivot man, instead of merely turning in his place, will conform himself to the movement of the marching flank, feel lightly the elbow of the next man, take steps of full nine inches, and thus gain ground forward so as to clear the point of the wheel. The middle of the rank will bend slightly to the rear. As soon as the movement shall commence, the man who conducts the marching flank will cast his eyes on the ground over which he will have to pass.

The wheel being ended, the instructor will command :

1. *Forward.* 2. MARCH.

The command forward will be given *four* paces before the wheel is complete.

At the command *march,* which will begin at the instant the wheel is complete, the man who conducts the wheel will march straight forward : the pivot man and all the rest of the squad will retake the step of twenty-eight inches, and bring the head direct to the front.

Turning, or change of direction to the side of the guide.

130. The change of direction to the side of the guide, in marching, will be executed as follows : the instructor will command :

1. *Left* (or *right turn.*) 2. MARCH.

The first command should be given when the squad is *four* paces from the turning point.

At the command *march,* to be pronounced at the instant the rank ought to turn, the guide will face to the left (or right) in marching, and move forward in the new direction without changing the pace. The whole squad will promptly conform to the new direction : to effect which, each man will advance the shoulder opposite the guide, take the double quick step, turn the head and eyes to the side of the guide, place himself on the line with the guide, from whom he will take the step, touch elbows to the side of the guide, and resume the direct position of the head.   The men will arrive in their places in regular succession.

131. When the men comprehend, and can execute the various wheels, etc., in quick time, the instructor will cause them to be repeated in double quick time, by the same commands, and according to same principles as in quick time, except that the command *double quick* will precede that of *march.* In wheeling while marching, the pivot man will take steps of eleven inches, and in the changes of direction to the side of the guide, the men on the side opposite the guide must increase the gait in order to bring themselves into line.

The instructor, in order not to fatigue the men, and not to divide their attention, will cause them to execute the several movements of wheelings, etc., first without arms, and next, after the mechanism be well comprehended, with arms.

SCHOOL OF THE COMPANY.
MANNER OF FORMING THE COMPANY.

132. The whole company being assembled on its parade ground, or in the rendezvous, the *first,* or orderly sergeant, will command:

Fall in—COMPANY.

At this command the corporals and privates will form in one rank, faced to the right, and in the order of height from right to left, the tallest man on the right (now head of the company), the next tallest man immediately covering the first, and so on to the left or rear of the rank, in which position will be placed the shortest man.   The other sergeants will take post in the rank of file closers, two paces to the right of the company, and assist the first sergeant in forming the company.

When the men have their places, the first sergeant will command :

FRONT.

The second sergeant, who is the left guide of the company, will now place himself on the left of the company, and the orderly sergeant will promptly command :

1. *In two ranks, form company.*   2. *left*—FACE 3. MARCH.

At the command *left face,* the whole company will face to the left, except the guide and man on the left, who stands fast.

At the command *march,* the whole of the men who have faced to the left, will step of together ; the second man counting from the left, will place himself in the rear rank, behind the man next to the guide, and face to the front: the two following men will, in like manner, on closing up, from the next file the third man in the front, and the fourth in the rear rank behind him, and all the other men will come successively to form files, two deep, to the right of those already formed.*

The officers will now take their posts as prescribed in No. 8† ; if the Captain has to discharge the duties of instructor, the first lieutenant will take his place on the right of the front rank, the second lieutenant replacing the first behind the fourth section.

The instructor will then cause the files to be numbered, and for this purpose will command :

In each rank—*count* TWOS.

At this command the men count in each rank from right to left, pronoun-

---

*When the company is in good discipline, the files may be formed in two ranks at once, each man having his proper number in the company depending upon his height, and being able to take his appropriate place without creating confusion.

† See "Army Organization" on last page.

cing in a loud and distinct voice, in the same tone, without hurry and without turning the head, *one, two,* according to the place each one occupies. He will also cause the company to be divided into platoons and sections, taking care that the first platoon is always composed of an even number of files.

To open ranks.

133. The company being at order arms, the ranks and file-closers well aligned, when the instructer shall wish to cause the ranks to be opened, he will direct the left guide to place himself on the left of the front rank, which being excuted, he will command :

1. *Company.* 2. *Shoulder—*Arms.

3. *To the rear, open order.*

At the last commaud, the covering seargeant (or orderly sergeant), and the left guide, will step off smartly to the rear, four paces of twenty-eight inches from the front rank, in order to mark the position for the rear rank. They will judge this reistance by the eye without counting the steps.

The instructor will place himself at the same time on the right flank, in order to observe if these two non-commissioned officers are on a line paralled to the front rank ; and, if necessary, to correct their positions, which being executed, he will commmand :

4. March.

At this command the front rank will stand fast. The rear rank will step to the rear without counting the steps, and place themselves on the alignment marked for this rank, each man stepping slightly behind the line, and then dressing forward as in the backward dress. The covering sergeant will dress the rear rank on the left guide placed to mark the left of this rank. The instructed seeing the rear rank aligned, will command :

5. Front.

At this command, the sergeant on the left of the rear rank will return to his place as a file-closer.

Alignments in open ranks.

134. The ranks being open, the inctructor will, in the first exercises, align the ranks, man by man, the better to inculcate the principles. To effect this, he will cause two or four men on the right or left of each rank to march two or three paces forward, and, after having aligned them, command :

*By file, right (or left) —*Dress.

At this, the men of each rank will move up successively on the alignment, each man being preceeded by his neighbor in the same rank, towards the basis, by two paces, and having correctly aligned himself, will cast his eyes to the front.

135. Successive alignments having habituated the soldier to dress correctly the instructor will cause the ranks to align themselves at once, forward and backward, sometimes in a direction paralled, and sometimes in one oblique to the original direction, giving, in each case, two or four men to servo as a basis of alignment to each rank- To effect which, he will command ;

1. *Right (or left) —*Dress. 2. Front :

or,

1 *Right (or left) backward—*Dress. 2. Front.

In oblique alignments, in opened ranks, the men of the rear rank will not seek to cover their file leaders, as the sole object of the exercise is to teach them to align themselves correctly in their respective ranks, in the different directions.

In the several alignments, the captain will superintend the front rank, and the covering sergeant the rear rank. For this purpose they will place themselves on the side by which the ranks are dressed.

In oblique alignments, the men will conform the line of their shoulders to the new direction of their ranks, and will place themselves on the alignment as has been prescribed in the school of the soldier, according as the new direction shall be in front or rear of the original one.

To close ranks.

136. The instructor will command:

1. *Close order.*   2. MARCH.

At the command *march*, the rear rank will close up in quick time, each man directing himself on his file leader.

Alignments in closed ranks.

137. The ranks being closed, the instructor will cause to be executed parallel and oblizued alignments by the rigot ond left, forward and backward, observing to place always two or four files as a basis of alignment.   He will give the same commands prescribed for *opened* ranks.

In alignments in closed ranks, the captain will superintend the front rank, and the covering sergeant the rear rank,   They will habituate themselves to judge the alignment by the lines of the eyes and shoulders, in casting a glance of the eye along the front and rear of the ranks.

The moment the captain preceives the greater number of the front rank aligned, he will command FRONT, and rectify afterwards, if necessary the alignment of the other man by ordering this or that file *forward or back*, designating each by its number.   Tue rear rank will conform to the alighment of the front rank, superintended by the covering sergeant.

The ranks being steady, the instructor will place himself on the flank to verify their alignment.   He will also see that each rear rank man covers accurately his file leader.

In all alignments, the file-closers will preserve the distance of two paces from the rear rank.

The alignments being ended the instructor will exercise the company at the manual, and finish with stacking arms as follows ;

To stack arms.

138. The men being at order arms, the instructor will command :

Stack—ARMS.

At this command, the front rank man of every even numbered file will pass his piece before him, seizing it with the left hand above the middle band, and place the butt behind and near the right foot of the next man on the left, the barrel turned to the front.   At the same time the front rank man of every odd numbered file will pass his piece before him, seizing it with the left hand below the middle band, and hand it to the man next on the left ; the latter will receive it with the right hand two inches above the middle band, throw the butt about thirty-two inches to the front, opposite to his right shoulder, incline the muzzle towards him, and lock the shanks of the two bayonets ; the lock of this second piece towards the right, and its shank above that of the first piece.   The rear rank man of every even file will project his bayonet forward, and introduce it (using both hands) between and under the shanks of the two other bayonets.   He will then abandon the piece to his file leader, who will receive it with the right hand under the middle band, bring the butt to the front, holding up his own piece and the stack with the left hand, and place the butt of this third piece between the feet of the man next on the right, the S plate to the rear.   The stack thus formed, the rear rank man of every odd file will pass his piece into his left hand, the barrel turned to the front, and, sloping the bayonet forward, rest it on the stack.

If the company be armed with *rifles*, or any piece without the bayonet, arms will be stacked by the same commands, and in the following manner : At the command *stack arms* the front rank man of every even numbered file will pass his piece before him, seizing it with the left hand near the upper band ; will place the butt a little in advance of his left toe, the barrel turned towards the body, and draw the rammer slightly from its place ; the front rank man of every odd numbered file will also draw the rammer slightly, and pass his piece to the man next on his left, who will seize it with the right hand near the upper band, and place the butt a little in advance of the right toe of the man next on the right, the barrel turned to the front ; he will then cross the rammers of the two pieces, the rammer of the piece of the odd numbered man being inside; the rear rank man of every even file will also draw his rammer, lean his piece forward, the lock plate downwards, advance the right foot about six inches, and insert the rammer between the rammer and barrel of the piece of his front rank man ; with his left hand he will place the butt of his piece on the ground, thirty-two inches in rear of, and perpendicular to, the front rank, bringing back his right foot by the side of his left; the front rank man of every even file will at the same time lean the stack to the rear, quit it with his right hand, and force all the rammers down. The stack being thus formed, the rear rank man of every odd file will pass his piece into his left hand, the barrel to the front, and inclining it forward, will rest it on the stack.

The men of both ranks having taken the position of the soldier without arms, the instructor will command :

1. *Break ranks.*   2. MARCH.

To Resume Arms.

139. Both ranks being re-formed in rear of their stacks, the instructor will command :

Take—ARMS.

At this command, the rear rank man of every odd numbered file will withdraw his piece from the stack ; the front rank man of every even file will seize his own piece with the left hand, and that of the man on his right hand, both above the lower band ; the rear rank man of the even file will seize his piece with the right hand below the lower band ; these two men will raise up the stock to loosen the rammers or bayonets; the front rank men of every odd file will facilitate the disengagement of the rammers, if necessary, by drawing them out slightly with the left hand, and will receive his piece from the hand of the man next on his left; the four men will retake the position of the soldier at order arms.

The firing.

To fire by company.

140. The instructor, wishing to cause the fire by company to be executed, will command :

1. *Fire by company.*   2. *Commence firing.*

At the first command, the captain will promptly place himself opposite the centre of his company, and four paces in rear of the line of file-closers ; the covering sergeant will retire to that line, and place himself opposite to his interval. *This rule is general, for both the captain and covering sergeant, in all the different firings.*

At the second command, the captain will add :

1. *Company.* 2. READY. 3. AIM. 4. FIRE. 5. LOAD.

At the command *load*, the men will load their pieces, and then take the position of *ready*, as prescribed in the school of the soldier.

The captain will immediately recommence the firing, by the commands :

1. *Company.* 2. AIM. 3. FIRE. 4. LOAD.

The firing will be thus continued until the signal to cease firing is sounded. The captain will sometimes cause aim to be taken to the right or left, simply observing to pronounce *right* (or *left*) *oblique*, before the command *aim*.

The fire by file.

141. The instructer wishing to cause the fire by file to be executed, will command :

    1. *Fire by file.* 2. *Company.* 3. READY. 4. *Commence firing*

The third and fourth commands will be executed as prescribed in the school of the soldier.

The fire will be commenced by the right file of the company ; the next file will take aim at the instant the first brings down pieces to reload, and so on to the left ; but this progression will only be observed in the first discharge, after which each man will reload and fire without regulating himself by others, conforming himself to what is prescribed in the school of the soldior.

The fire by rank.

142. The instructer wishing the fire by rank to be executed, will command :

    1. *Fire by rank.* 2. *Company.* 3. READY. 4. *Rear rank*—AIM. 5. FIRE.
        6. LOAD.

The fifth and sixth commands will be executed as is prescribed in the school of the soldier.

When the instructor sees one or two pieces in the rear rank at a ready, he will command :

    1. *Front rank.* 2. AIM. 3. FIRE. 4. LOAD.

The firing will commence thus by alternate ranks, until the signal is given to cease firing.

143. The instructor will sometimes cause aim to be taken to the right and left, conforming to what is prescribed for the oblique fire.

The instructor will cause the firing to cease, whether by company, by file, or by rank, by sounding the signal to *cease firing ;* at which signal the men will cease to fire. If they have fired, they will load their pieces and bring them to a shoulder ; if at the position of *ready,* they will half cock and shoulder arms. If in the position of *aim,* they will bring down their pieces half-cock, and shoulder arms.

144. The signal to cease firing will be always followed by a bugle note, or tap of the drum ; at which sound the captain and covering sergeant will promptly resume their places in line, and will rectify, if necessary, the alignment of the ranks.

The fire by file being that which is most frequently used against an enemy, it is highly important that it be rendered perfectly familiar to the troops. The instructor will, therefore, give it almost exclusive preference, and labor to cause the men to aim with care, and always, if possible, at some particular object. As it is of the utmost importance that the men should aim with precision in battle, this principle will be rigidly enforced in the exercise for purposes of instruction.

To fire by the rear rank.

145. The instructor will cause the several fires to be executed to the rear, that is, by the rear rank. To effect this he will command :

    1. *Face by the rear rank.* 2. *Company.* 3. *About.*—FACE.

At the first command, the captain will step out and place himself near to, and facing the right file of his company ; the covering sergeant and file-closers will pass quickly through the captain's interval, and place themselves faced to the rear, the covering sergeant a pace behind the captain, and the file-closers two paces from the front rank opposite to their places in line, each passing behind the covering sergeant.

At the third command, which will be given at the instant the last file-closer shall have passed through the interval, the company will face about ; the captain will place himself in his interval in the rear rank, now become the front, and the covering sergeant will cover him in the front rank, now become the rear.

The company having faced by the rear rank, the instructor will cause it to execute the fire by company, both direct and oblique, the fire by file, and the fire by rank, by the commands and means proscribed. The captain, covering sergeant, and the men will conform themselves, in like manner, to what is prescribed.

The fire by file will commence on the left of the company, now become the right. In the fire by rank the firing will commence with the front rank, now become the rear.

To resume the proper front, the instructor will command:

1. *Face by the front rank.* 2. *Company.* 3. *About.* 4. FACE.

At the first command, the captain, covering sergeant, and file-closers will conform to what is prescribed above.

At the third command, the company having faced about, the captain and covering sergeant will resume their place in line.

In this lesson, the instructor will impress on the men the importance of aiming always at some particular object, and of holding the piece as prescribed in the school of the soldier.

The instructor will recommend to the captain to make a short pause between the commands *aim* and *fire*, to give the men time to aim with accuracy.

To advance in line of battle.

146. The company being in line of battle, and correctly aligned, when the instructor shall wish to exercise it in marching by the front, he will assure himself that the shoulders of the captain and covering sergeant are perfectly in the direction of their respective ranks, and that the sergeant accurately covers the captain; the instructor will then place himself twenty-five or thirty paces in front of them, face to the rear, and to place himself exactly on the prolongation of the line passing between their heels.

The instructor, being aligned on the directing file, will command:

Company, forward.

At this, a sergeant, previously designated, will move six paces in advance of the captain: the instructor, from the position prescribed, will correctly align this sergeant on the prolongation of the directing file.

This advanced sergeant who is to be charged with the direction, will, the moment his position is assured, take two points on the ground in the straight line which would pass between his own and the heels of the instructor.

These dispositions being made, the instructor will step aside, and command:

2. MARCH.

At this, the company will step off with life. The directing sergeant will observe, with the greatest precision, the length and cadence of the step, marching on the two points he has chosen; he will take in succession, and always a little before arriving at the point nearest to him, new points in advance, exactly in the same line with the first two, and at the distance of some fifteen or twenty paces from each other. The captain will march steadily in the trace of the directing sergeant, keeping always six paces from him; the men will each maintain the head direct to the front, feel lightly the elbow of his neighbor on the side of direction, and conform himself to the principles prescribed, school of the soldier, for the march by the front.

The man next to the captain will take special care not to pass him: to this end, he will keep the line of his shoulders a little in the rear, but in the same direction with those of the captain.

The file-closers will march at the habitual distance of two paces behind the rear rank.

If the men loose the step, the instructor will command:

To the—STEP.

At this command, the men will glance towards the directing sergeant, retake the step from him, and again direct their eyes to the front.

The instructor will cause the captain and covering sergeant to be posted sometimes on the right, and sometimes on the left of the company.

The directing sergeant, in advance, having the greatest influence on the march of the company, he will be selected for the precision of his step, his habit of maintaining his shoulders in a square with a given line of direction, and of prolonging that line without variation.

To halt the Company, in marching in line of battle, and to align it.

The instructor, wishing to halt the company, will command :

1. *Company.* 2. HALT.

At the second command, the company will halt; the directing sergeant will remain in advance, unless ordered to return to the line of file-closers. The company being at a halt, the instructor may advance the first three or four files on the side of direction, and align the company on that basis, or he may confine himself to causing the alignment to be rectified. In this last case, he will command: *Captain, rectify the alignment.* The captain will direct the covering sergeant to attend to the rear rank, when each, glancing his eyes along his rank, will promptly rectify it, conforming to what is prescribed in the school of the soldier.

Oblique march in line of battle.

147. The company being in the direct march, when the instructor shall wish to cause it to march obliquely, he will command:

1. *Right* (or *left*) *oblique.* 2. MARCH.

At the command *march*, the company will take the oblique step. The men will accurately observe the principles prescribed in the school of the soldier. The rear rank men will preserve their distances, and march in rear of the man next on the right (or left) of their habitual file leaders.

When the instructor wishes the direct march to be resumed, he will command :

1. *Forward.* 2. MARCH.

At the command *march*, the company will resume the direct march. The instructor will move briskly twenty paces in front of the captain, and facing the company, will place himself exactly in the prolongation of the captain and covering sergeant ; and then, by a sign, will move the directing sergent on the same line, if he be not already on it; the latter will immediately take two points on the ground between himself and the instructor, and as he advances, will take new points of direction.

In the oblique march, the men not having the touch of elbows, the guide will always be on the side towards which the oblique is made, without any indication to that effect being given ; and when the direct march is resumed, the guide will be, equally without indication, on the side where it was previous to the oblique.

To mark time, to march in double quick time, and the back step.

148. The company being in the direct march and in quick time, the instructor, to cause it to mark time, will command :

1. *Mark time.* 2. MARCH.

To resume the march, he will command :

1. *Forward.* 2. MARCH.

To cause the march in double quick time, the instructor will command :

1. *Double quick.* 2. MARCH.

The command *march* will be pronounced at the instant either foot is coming to the ground.

To resume quick time, the instructor will command :

1. *Quick time.* 2. March.

The command *march* will be pronounced at the instant either foot is coming to the ground.

The company being at a halt; the instructor may cause it to march in the back step ; to this effect, he will command :

1. *Company backward.* 2. March.

The back step will bo executed according to the principles prescribed in the school of ho soldier, but the use of it being rare, the instructor will not cause more than fifteen er twenty steps to be taken in succession, and to that extent but seldom.

Tho instructor ought not to exercise the company in marching in double quick time till the men are well established in the length and swiftness of the pace in quick time ; ho will then endeavor to render the march of 165 steps in the minute equally easy and familiar. and also cause them to observe tho same erectness of body and composure of mind, as if marching in quick time.

To march in retreat.

149. The company being halted and correctly aligned, when the instructor shall wish to cause it to march in retreat, he will command :

1. *Company.* 2. *About.* Face.

The company having faced to the rear, the instructor will place himself in front of the directing file.

The instructor being correctly, established on the prolongation of the directing file, will command :

3. *Company, forward.*

At this, the directing sergeant will conform himself to what is prescribed No. 146, with this difference—he will place himself six paces in front of the line of file-closers, now leading.

The covering sergeant will step into the line of file closers; opposite to his interval, and the captain will place himself in the rear rank, now become tho front.

This disposition being promptly made, the instructor will command :

4. March,

At this, the directing sergeant, the captain, and the men, will conform themselves to what is prescribed No, 146.

The instructor will cause to be executed, marching in retreat, all that is prescribed for marching in advance ; the commands and the means of execution will be the same.

The instructor having halted the company, will, when he may wish, cause it to face to the front. The captain, the covering sergeant, and the directing sergeant, will resume their habitual places in line, tho moment they shall have faced about.

150. The company being in march by the front rank, if the instructor should wish it to march in retreat, he will cause the right about to be executed while marching, and to this effect will command :

1. *Company.* 2. *Right about.* 3. March.

At the third command, the company will promptly face about, and recommence tho march by the rear rank.

The directing sergeant will face about with the company, and will move rapidly six paces in front of the file-closers, and upon the prolongation of the guide. The instructor will place him in the proper direction by the means prescribed. The captain, the covering sergeant, and the men, will conform to the principles prescribed for the march in retreat.

When the instructor wishes the company to march by the front rank, he will give the same commands, and will regulate the direction of the march by the same means.

151. The instructor will cause all the above marches, except the backward march, to be executed in the double quick time; the latter will be executed only in quick time. He will give the same commands, observing to add *double quick* before the command *march*.

When the pieces are carried on the right shoulder, in quick time, the distance between the ranks will be sixteen inches. Whenever, therefore, the instructor brings the company from a shoulder to this position, the rear rank must shorten a little the first steps in order to gain the prescribed distance, and will lengthen the steps on the contrary, in order to close up when the pieces are again brought to a shoulder. In marching in double quick time, the distance between the ranks will be twenty six inches, and the pieces will be carried habitually on the right shoulder.

Whenever a company is halted, the men will bring their pieces at once to a shoulder at the command *halt*. The rear rank will close to its proper distance. *These rules are general.*

To march by the flank.

152. The company being in line of battle, and at a halt, when the instructor shall wish to cause it to march by the right flank, he will command :

1. *Company, right*—FACE. 2. *Forward.* 3. MARCH.

At the first command, the company will face to the right, the covering sergeant will place himself at the head of the front rank, the captain having stepped out for the purpose, so far as to find himself by the side of the sergeant, and on his left; the two ranks will form to the right at the word, the rear rank will step off one pace to the right, then the even numbers of both ranks will step up to the right of the odd, as directed in the school of the soldier; so that when the movement is completed, the files will be formed of four men aligned, and elbow to elbow. The intervals will be preserved.

The file closers will also move by side step to the right, so that when the ranks are formed, they will be two paces from the raremost rank.

At the command *march*, the company will move off briskly in quick time; the covering sergeant at the head of the front rank, and the captain on his left will march straight forward. The men of each file will march abreast of their respective front rank men, heads direct to the front; the file-closers will march opposite their places in line of battle.

The instructor will cause the march by the left flank to be executed by the same commands, substituting left for right; the rear rank steps one pace to the left, then the odd files of both ranks take their places to the left of the even numbered.

At the instant the company faces to the left, the left guide will place himself at the head of the front rank, the captain will pass rapidly to the left, and place himself by the right side of his guide; the covering sergeant will replace the captain in the front rank, the moment the latter quits it to go to the left.

The instructor will sometimes exercise the company in facing without doubling, for this purpose he will command :

1. *Company, in two ranks, right*—2. FACE.

The *double quick*, however, will never be executed without the ranks being doubled.

To change direction by file.

153. The company being faced by the flank, and either in march, or at a halt, when the instructor shall wish to cause it to wheel by file, he will command :

1. *By file left* (or *right.*)   2. MARCH.

At the command *march*, the first file will wheel ; if to the side of the front rank man, the latter will take care not to turn at once, but to describe a short arc of a circle, shortening a little the first five or six steps in order to give time to the fourth man of this file to conform himself to the movement. If the wheel be to the side of the rear rank, the front rank man will wheel in the step of twenty-eight inches, and the fourth man will conform himself to the movement by describing a short arc of a circle as has been explained. Each file will come to wheel on the same ground where that which preceded it wheeled.

The instructor will see that the wheel be executed according to these principles, in order that the distance between the files may always be preserved, and that there be no check or hindrance at the wheeling point.

1. *To halt the company marching by the flank, and to face it to the front.*

154 To effect these objects, the instructor will command :

1. *Company.*   2. HALT   3. FRONT.

The second and third commands will be executed as prescribed in the school of the soldier. As soon as the files have undoubled the rear rank will close to its proper distance. The captain and covering sergeant, as well as the left guide; if the march be by the left flank, will return to their habitual places in line at the instant the company faces to the front.

The instructor may then align the company by one of the means prescribed.

1. *The company being in march by the flank, to form it on the right* (or *left*) *by file into line of battle.*

155. If the company be marching by the right flank; the instructor will command :

1. *On the right by file into line.*   2. MARCH.

At the command *march*, the rear rank men doubled will mark time ; the captain and covering sergeant will turn to the right, march straight forward, and be halted by the instructor when they shall have passed at least six paces beyond the rank of file-closers ; the captain will place himself correctly on the line of battle, and will direct the alignment as the men of the front rank successively arrive ; the covering sergeant will place himself behind the captain at the distance of the rear rank ; the two men on the right of the front rank doubled, will continue to march, and passing beyond the covering sergeant and the captain, will turn to the right; after turning, they will continue to march elbow to elbow, and direct themselves towards the line of battle, but when they shall arrive at two pace, from this line; the even number will shorten the step so that the odd number may precede him on the line, the odd number placing himself by the side and on the left side of the captain ; the even number will afterwards oblique to the left, and place himself on the left of the odd number : the next two men of the front rank doubled, will pass in the same manner behind the two first, turn then to the right, and place themselves, according to the means just explained, to the left, and by the side of, the two men already established on the line ; the remaining files of this rank will follow in succession, and be formed to the left in the same manner. The rear rank doubled will execute the movement in the manner already explained for the front rank, taking care not to commence the movement until four men of the front rank are established on the line of battle ; the rear rank men, as they arrive on the line, will cover accurately their file leaders.

If the company be marching by the left flank, the instructor will cause it to form by file on the left into line of battle, according to the same principles and by the same commands, substituting the indication *left* for *right* In this case, the odd numbers will shorten the step, so that the even numbers may precede them on the line. The captain, placed on the left of the front rank, and the left guide, will return to their places in line of battle, by order of the instructor, after the company shall be formed and aligned.

To enable the men the better to comprehend the mechanism of this movement, the instructor will at first cause it to be executed separately by each rank doubled, and afterwards by the two ranks united and doubled.

The company being in march by the flank, to form it by company, or platoon, into line, and to cause it to face to the right and left in marching.

156. The company being in march by the right flank, the instructor will order the captain to form it into line; the captain will immediately command:

1. *By company into line.* 2. MARCH.

At the command *march*, the covering sergeant will continue to march straight forward; the men will advance the right shoulder, take the double quick step, and move into line by the shortest route, taking care to undouble the files, and to come on the line after the other.

As the front rank men successively arrive in line with the covering sergeant, they will take from him the step, and then turn their eyes to the front.

The men of the rear rank will conform to the movements of their respective file leaders, but without endeavoring to arrive in line at the same time with the latter.

At the instant the movement begins, the captain will face to his company in order to follow up the execution; and, as soon as the company is formed, he will command, *guide left*, place himself two paces before the centre, face to the front, and take the step of the company.

At the command *guide left*, the second sergeant will promptly place himself in the front rank, on the left, to serve as guide, and the covering sergeant who is on the oppposite flank will remain there.

When the company marches by the left flank, this movement will be executed by the same commands, and according to the same principles; the company being formed, the captain will command *guide right*, and place himself in front of his company as above; the covering sergeant who is on the right of the front rank will serve as guide, and the second sergeant placed on the left flank will remain there.

Thus, supposing the company to constitute a part of a column by company, right or left in front, the covering sergeant and the second sergeant of each company will always be placed on the right and left, respectively, of the front rank; they will be denominated *right guide* and *left guide*, and the one or the other charged with the direction.

The company being in march by the flank, if it be the wish of the instructor to cause it to form platoons, he will give an order to that effect to the captain, who will command.

1. *By platoon into line.* 2. MARCH.

The movement will be executed by each platoon according to the above principles. The captain will place himself before the centre of the first platoon, and the first lieutenant before the centre of the second, passing through the opening made in the centre of the company, if the march be by the right flank, and around the left of his platoon, if the march be by the left; in this last case the captain will also pass around the left of the second platoon in order to place himself in front of the first. Both the captain and lieutenant, without waiting for each other, will command *guide left* (or *right*) at the instant their respective platoons are formed.

At the command *guide left* (or *right*), the guide of each platoon will pass rapidly to the indicated flank of the platoon, if not already there.

The right guide of the company will always serve as the guide of the right or left of the first platoon, and the left guide of the company will serve, in like manner, as the guide of the second platoon.

Thus in a column, by platoon, there will be but one guide to each platoon. he will always be placed on its left flank, if the right be in front, and on the right flank, if the left be in front.

In these movements the file-closers will follow the platoons to which they are attached.

The instructor may cause the company, marching by the flank, to form by company or platoon, into line, by his own direct commands, using those prescribed for the captain.

The instructor will exercise the company in passing, without halt, from the march by the front, to the march by the flank, and reciprocally. In either case, he will employ the commands prescribed in the school of the soldier, substituting *company* for *squad*. The company will face to the right or left, in marching, and the captain, the guides, and file-closers will conform themselves to what is prescribed for each in the march by the flank, or in the march by the front of the company supposed to be a sub-division of a column.

If, after facing to the right or left, in marching, the company find itself faced by the rear rank, the captain will place himself two paces behind the centre of the front rank, now in the rear, the guides will pass to the rear rank, now leading, and the file closers will march in front of this rank.

The instructor, in order to avoid fatiguing the men, and to prevent them from being negligent in the position of shoulder arms, will sometimes order support arms in marching by the flank, and arms on the right shoulder, when marching in line

To break into column by platoon, either at a halt or in march.

157. The company being at a halt, in line of battle, the instructor, wishing to break it into column, by platoon to the right, will command:

1. *By platoon, right wheel.* 2. MARCH.

At the first command, the chiefs of platoons will rapidly place themselves two paces before the centres of their respective platoons, the lieutenant passing around the left of the company. They need not occupy themselves with dressing, one upon the other. The covering sergeant will replace the captain in the front rank.

At the command *march*, the right front rank man of each platoon will face to the right, the covering sergeant standing fast, the chief of each platoon will move quickly by the shortest line, a little beyond the point at which the marching flank will rest when the wheel shall be completed, face to the late rear, and place himself so that the line which he forms with the man on the right (who had faced). shall be perpendicular to that occupied by the company in line of battle; each platoon will wheel according to the principles prescribed for the wheel on a fixed pivot, and when the man who conducts the marching flank shall approach near to the perpendicular, its chief will command:

1. *Platoon.* 2. HALT.

At the command *halt*, which will be given at the instant the man who conducts the marching flank shall have arrived at three paces from the perpendicular, the platoon will halt; the covering sergeant will move to the point where the left of the first platoon is to rest, passing by the front rank; the second sergeant will place himself, in like manner, in respect to the second platoon. Each will take care to leave between himself and the man on the right of his platoon, a space equal to its front; the captain and first lieutenant will look to this, and each take care to align the sergeant between himself and the man of the platoon who had faced to the right.

The guide of each platoon, being thus established on the perpendicular, each chief will place himself two paces outside of his guide, and facing towards him, will command :

3. *Left*—DRESS.

The alignment being ended, each chief of platoon will command, FRONT, and place himself two paces before its centre.

The file-closers will conform themselves to the movement of their respective platoons, preserving always the distance of two paces from the rear rank.

The company will break by platoon to the left,, according to the same principles. The instructor will command :

1. *By platoon, left wheel.* 2. MARCH.

The first command will be executed in the same manner as if breaking by platoon to the right.

At the command *march*, the left front rank man of each platoon will face to the left, and the platoon will wheel to the left, according to the principles prescribed for the wheel on a fixed pivot ; the chiefs of platoon will conform to the principles indicated.

At the command *halt*, given by the chief of each platoon, the covering sergeant on the right of the front rank of the first platoon, and the second sergeant near the left of the second platoon, will each move to the points where the right of his platoon is to rest. The chief of each platoon should be careful to align the sergeant and himself and the man of the platoon who had faced to the left, and will then command :

Right—DRESS.

The platoons being aligned, each chief of platoon will command; FRONT, and place himself opposite its centre.

158. The instructor wishing to break the company by platoon to the right, and to move the column forward after the wheel is completed, will caution the company to that effect, and command :

1. *By platoon, right wheel.* 2. MARCH.

At the first command, the chiefs of platoon will move rapidly in front of their respective platoons, conforming to what has been prescribed, and will remain in this position during the continuance of the wheel. The covering sergeant will replace the chief of the first platoon in the front rank.

At the command *march*, the platoons will wheel to the right, conforming to the principles herein prescribed ; the man on the pivot will not face to the right, but will mark time, conforming himself to the movement of the marching flank ; and when the man who is on the left of this flank shall arrive near the perpendicular, the instructor will command :

3. *Forward.* 4. MARCH. 5. *Guide left*

At the fourth command, which will be given at the instant the wheel is completed, the platoons will move straight to the front, all the men taking the step of twenty-eight inches. The covering sergeant and the second sergeant will move rapidly to the left of their respective platoons, the former passing before the front rank. The leading guide will immediately take points on the ground in the direction which may be indicated to him by the instructor.

At the fifth command, the men will take the touch of elbows lightly to the left.

If the guide of the second platoon should loose his distance, or the line of direction, he will conform to the principles herein prescribed.

If the company be marching in line to the front, the instructor will cause it to break by platoon to the right by the same commands. At the command *march*, the platoons will wheel in the manner already explained ; the man on the pivot will take care to mark time in his place, without advancing or

At the command *march*, given by the captain, the second platoon will begin to mark time ; its chief will immediately add :

1. *Right oblique.* 2. MARCH.

The last command will be given so that this platoon may commence obliquing the instant the rear rank of the first platoon shall have passed. The men will shorten the step in obliquing, so that when the command *forward march* is given, the platoon may have its exact distance.

The guide of the second platoon being near the direction of the guide of the first, the chief of the second will command *Forward*, and add MARCH, the instant that the guide of his platoon shall cover the guide of the first.

In a column, left in front, the company will break into platoons by inverse means, applying to the first platoon all that has been prescribed for the second, and reciprocally.

In this case, the left guide of the company will shift to the right flank of the second platoon, and the covering sergeant will remain on the right of the first.

The column by platoon, being in march, right in front, when the instructor shall wish to cause it to form company, he will give the order to the captain, who will command :

Form company.

Having given this command, the captain will immediately add :

1. *First platoon.* 2. *Right oblique.*

The chief of the second platoon will caution it to continue to march straight forward.

The captain will then command :

3. MARCH.

At this command, repeated by the chief of the second, the first platoon will oblique to the right, in order to unmask the second ; the covering sergeant, on the left of the first platoon, will return to the right of the company, passing by the front rank.

When the first platoon shall have nearly unmasked the second, the captain will command :

1. *Mark time.*

and at the instant the unmasking shall be complete, he will add :

2. MARCH.

The first platoon will then cease to oblique, and mark time.

In a column, left in front, the same movement will be executed by inverse means, the chief of the second platoon giving the command *Forward*, and at the instant the two platoons shall unite, add MARCH : the first platoon will then cease to mark time.

In a column, left in front, the same movement will be executed by inverse means, the chief of the second platoon, giving the command *Forward*, and the captain adding the command MARCH, when the platoons are united The guide of the second platoon, on its right, will pass to its left flank the moment the platoon begins to oblique ; the guide of the first, on its right remaining on that flank of the platoon.

The instructor will also sometimes cause the company to break and reform, by platoon, by his own direct commands. In this case, he will give the general commands prescribed for the captain above :

1. *Break into platoons.* 2. MARCH.

and,

1. *Form company.* 2. MARCH.

If, in breaking the company into platoons, the subdivision that breaks off should mark time too long, it might, in a column of many subdivisions, arrest the march of the following one, which would cause a lengthening of the column, and a loss of distances.

Being in column, to break files to the rear, and to cause them to re-enter into line.

165. The company being in march, and supposed to constitute a subdivision of a column, right (or left) in front, when the instructor shall wish to cause files to break off he will give the order to the captain, who will immediately turn to his company,. and command :

1. *Two files from left* (or *right*) *to rear.* 2. MARCH.

At the command *march*, the two files on the left (or right) of the company will mark time, the others will continue to mach straight forward ; the two rear rank men of these files will, as soon as the rear rank of the company shall clear them, move to the right by advancing the outer shoulder ; the odd number will place himself behind the third file from that flank, the even number behind the fourth, passing for this purpose behind the odd number ; the two front rank men will, in like manner, move to the right when the rear rank of the company shall clear them, the odd number will place himself behind the first file, the even number behind the second file, passing for this purpose behind the odd number. If the files are broken from the right, the men will move to the left, advancing the outer shoulder, the even number of the rear rank will place himself behind the third file, the odd number of the same rank behind the fourth ; the even number of the front rank behind the first file, the odd number of the same rank behind the second, the odd numbers for this purpose passing behind the even numbers. The men will be careful not to lose their distances, and to keep aligned.

If the instructor should still wish to break two files from the same side, he will give the order to the captain, who will proceed as above directed.

At the command *march*, given by the captain, the files already broken, advancing a little the outer shoulder, will gain the space of two files to the right, if the files are broken from the left, and to the left, if the files are broken from the right, shortening, at the same time, the step, in order to make room between themselves and the rear rank of the company for the files last ordered to the rear ; the latter will break by the same commands and in the same manner as the first. The men who double should increase the length of the step in order to prevent distances from being lost.

The instructor may thus diminish the front of a company by breaking off successive groups of two files, but the new files must always be broken from the same side.

The instructor, wishing to cause files broken off to return into line, will give the order to the captain, who will immediately command :

1. *Two files into line.* 2. MARCH.

At the command *march*, the first two files of those marching by the flank, will return briskly into line, and the others will gain the space of two files by advancing the inner shoulder towards the flank to which they belong.

The captain will turn to his company, to watch the observance of the principles which have just been prescribed.

The instructor having caused groups of two files to break one after another, and to return again into line, will afterwards cause two or three groups to break together, and for this purpose, will command : *Four or six files from left* (or *right*) *to rear ;* MARCH. The files designated will mark time ; each rank will advance a little the outer shoulder as soon as the rear rank of the company shall clear it, will oblique at once, and each group will place itself behind the four neighboring files, and in the same manner, as if the movement had been executed group by group, taking care that the distances are preserved.

The instructor will next order the captain to cause two or three groups to be brought into line at once, who turning to the company, will command :

*Four or six files into line—*MARCH.

At the command *march,* the files designated will advance the inner shoulder, move up and form on the flank of the company by the shortest lines.

As often as files shall break off to the rear, the guide on that flank will gradually close on the nearest front rank man remaining in line, and he will also open out to make room for files ordered into line.

The files which march in the rear are disposed in the following order: the left files as if the company was marching by the right flank, and the right files as if the company was marching by the left flank. Consequently, whenever there is on the right or left of a subdivision, a file which does not belong to a group, it will be broken singly.

It is necessary to the preservation of distances in column that the men should be habituated in the schools of detail to execute the movement of this article with precision.

If new files broken off do not step well to the left or right in obliquing; if, when files are ordered into line, they do not move up with promptitude and precision, in either case the following files will be arrested in their march, and thereby cause the column to be lengthened out.

The instructor will place himself on the flank from which the files are broken, to assure himself of the exact observance of the principles.

Files will only be broken off from the side of direction, in order that the whole company may easily pass from the front to the flank march.

To march the column in route, and to execute the movements incident thereto.

166. The swiftness of the route step will be 110 steps in a minute; this swiftness will be habitually maintained in column in route, when the roads and ground may permit.

The company being at a halt, and supposed to constitute a subdision of a column, when the instructor shall wish to cause it to march in the route step, he will command:

1. *Column, forward.* 2. *Guide, left* (or *right*). 3. *Route step.* 4. MARCH.

At the command *march,* repeated by the captain, the two ranks will step off together; the rear rank will take, in marching, by shortening a few steps, a distance of one pace (twenty-eight inches) from the rank preceding, which distance will be computed from the breasts of the men in the rear rank, to the knapsacks of the men in the front rank. The men, without further command, will immediately carry their arms *at will,* as indicated in the school of the soldier. They will no longer be required to march in the cadenced space, or with the same foot, or to remain silent. The files will march at ease: but care will be taken to prevent the ranks from intermixing, the front rank from getting in advance of the guide, and the rear rank from opening to too great a distance.

The company marching in the route step, the instructor will cause it to change direction, which will be executed without formal commands, on a simple caution from the captain; the rear rank will come up to change direction in the same manner as the front rank. Each rank will conform itself, although in the route step, to the principles which have been prescribed for the change in closed ranks, with this difference only; that the pivot man, instead of taking steps of nine, will take stops of fourteen inches, in order to clear the wheeling point.

The company marching in the route step, to cause it to pass to the cadenced step, the instructor will first order pieces to be brought to the shoulder, and then command:

1. *Quick time.* 2. MARCH.

At the command *march,* the men will resume the cadenced step, and will close so as to leave a distance of sixteen inches between each rank.

167. The company marching in the cadenced pace, the instructor, to cause it to take the route step will command :

1. *Route step.* 2. MARCH.

At the command *march*, the front rank will continue the step of twenty-eight inches, the rear rank will take, by gradually shortening the step, the distance of twenty-eight inches from the front rank ; the men will carry their arms at will.

The instructor will exercise the company in increasing and diminishing front, by platoon, which will be executed by the same commands, and the same means, as if the company were marching in the cadenced step. When the company breaks into platoons, the chief of each will move to the flank of his platoon, and will take the place of the guide, who will step back into the rear rank.

168. The company being in column, by platoon, and marching in the route step, the instructor can cause the front to be diminished and increased, by section, if the platoons have a front of twelve files or more.

The movements of diminishing and increasing front, by section, will be executed according to the principles indicated for the same movement by platoon. The right sections of platoons will be commanded by the captain and first lieutenant, respectively ; the left sections, by the two next subaltern in rank, or, in their absence, by sergeants.

The instructor wishing to diminish by section, will give the order to the captain, who will command :

1. *Break into sections.* 2. MARCH.

As soon as the platoons shall be broken, each chief of section will place himself on its directing flank in the front rank, the guides who will be thus displaced, will fall back into the rear rank ; the file-closers will close up to within one pace of this rank.

Platoons will be broken into sections only in the column in route, the movement will never be executed in the manoeuvres, whatever may be the front of the company.

When the instructor shall wish to re-form platoons, he will give the order to the captain, who will command :

1. *Form platoons.* 2. MARCH.

At the first command, each chief of section will place himself before its centre, and the guides will pass into the front rank. At the command *march*, the movement will be executed as has been prescribed for forming company. The moment the platoons are formed, the chiefs of the left sections will return to their places as file-closers.

The instructor will also cause to be executed the disminishing and increasing front by files, as prescribed in the preceding article, and in the same manner, as if marching in the cadenced step. When the company is broken into section, the subdivisions must not be reduced to a front of less than six files, not counting the chief of the section.

The company being broken by platoon, or by section, the instructor will cause it, marching in the route step, to march by the flank in the same direction, by the commands and the means indicated. The moment the subdivisions shall face to the right (or left,) the first file of each will wheel to the left (or right,) in marching, to prolong the direction, and to unite with the rear file of the subdivision immediately preceding. The file-closers will take their habitual places in the march by the flank, before the union of the subdivisions.

169. If the company be marching by the right flank, and the instructor should wish to undouble the files, which might sometimes be found necessary, he will inform the ca⸱ ⸱ ⸱ ⸱ after causing the cadenced step to be resumed, and arms to be ⸱ ⸱ ⸱ ⸱ ⸱ ⸱ ⸱ nand :

1. *In two ranks, undouble files.* 2. MARCH.

At the second command, the odd numbers will continue to march straight forward, the even numbers will shorten the step, and obliquing to the left will place themselves promptly behind the odd numbers; the rear rank will gain a step to the left so as to re-take the touch of elbows on the side of the front rank.

If the company be marching by the left flank, it will be the even numbers who will continue to march forward, and the odd numbers who will undouble.

If the instructor should wish to double the files, he will give the order to the captain, who will command:

1. *In four ranks, double files.* 2. MARCH.

At the command *march*, the files will double in the manner as explained, when the company faces by the right or left flank. The instructor will afterwards cause the route step to be resumed.

The various movements prescribed in this lesson may be executed in double quick time. The men will be brought, by degrees, to pass over at this gait about 1100 yards in seven minutes.

When the company marching in the route step shall halt, the rear rank will close up at the command *halt,* and the whole will shoulder arms.

Marching in the route step, the men will be permitted to carry their pieces in the manner they shall find most convenient, paying attention only to holding the muzzles up, so as to avoid accidents.

Countermarch.

170. The company being at a halt, and supposed to constitute a part of a column, right in front, when the instructor shall wish to cause it to counter-march, he will command:

1. *Countermarch.* 2. *Company right*—FACE. 3. *By file left.* 4. MARCH.

At the second command, the company will face to the right, the two guides to the right about; the captain will go to the right of his company and cause two files to break to the rear, and then place himself by the side of the front rank man, to conduct him.

At the command *march*, both guides will stand fast; the company will step off smartly; the first file, conducted by the captain, will wheel around the right guide, and direct its march along the front rank so as to arrive behind, and two paces from the left guide; each file will come in succession to wheel on the same ground around the right guide; the leading file having arrived at a point opposite to the left guide, the captain will command:

1. *Company.* 2. HALT. 3. FRONT. 4. *Right*—DRESS.

The first command will be given at *four* paces from the point where the leading file is to rest.

At the second command, the company will halt.

At the third, it will face to the front.

At the fourth, the company will dress by the right; the captain will step two paces outside of the left guide, now on the right, and direct the align-ment, so that the front rank may be enclosed between the two guides: the company being aligned, he will command FRONT, and place himself before the centre of the company as if in column: the guides, passing along the front rank, will shift to their proper places, on the right and left of that rank.

In a column, by platoon, the countermarch will be executed by the same commands, and according to the same principles; the guide of each platoon will face about, and its chief will place himself by the side of the file on the right, to conduct it.

In a column, left in front, the countermarch will be executed by inverse commands and means, but according to the same principles. Thus, the movement will be made by the right flank of subdivisions, if the right be in front; and by the left flank, if the left be in front; in both cases the subdivisions will wheel by file to the side of the front rank.

Being in column by platoon, to form on the right (or *left*) *into line of battle.*

171. The column by platoon, right in front, being in march, the instructor wishing to form it on the right into line of battle, will command:

    1. *On the right into line.* 2. *Guide right.*

At the second command, the guide of each platoon will shift quickly to its right flank, and the men will touch elbows to the right; the column will continue to march straight forward.

The instructor having given the second command, will move briskly to the point at which the right of the company ought to rest in line, and place himself facing the point of direction to the left which he will choose.

The line of battle ought to be so chosen that the guide of each platoon, after having turned to the right, may have at least ten paces to take before arriving upon that line.

The Lead of the column being nearly opposite to the instructor, the chief of the first platoon will command: 1. *Right turn;* and when exactly opposite to that point, he will add:

    2. MARCH.

At the command *march*, the first platoon will turn to the right, in conformity with the principles prescribed in the school of the soldier. Its guide will so direct his march as to bring the front rank man next on his left opposite to the instructor; the chief of the platoon will march before its centre; and when its guide shall be near the line of battle, he will command:

    1. *Platoon.* 2. *Halt.*

At the command *halt*, which will be given at the instant the right of the platoon shall arrive at the distance of three paces from the line of battle the platoon will halt: the files not yet in line will come up promptly. The guide will throw himself on the line of battle, opposite to one of the three left files of his platoon; he will face to the instructor, who will align him on the point of direction to the left. The chief of platoon having, at the same time, gone to the point where the right of the company is to rest, will, as soon as he sees all the files of the platoon in line, command:

    *Right—*DRESS.

At this, the first platoon will align itself; the front rank man, who finds himself opposite to the guide, will rest his breast lightly against the right arm of this guide, and the chief of the platoon, from the right, will direct the alignment on this man.

The second platoon will continue to march straight forward, until its guide shall arrive opposite to the left file of the first; it will then turn to the right at the command of its chief, and march towards the line of battle, its guide directing himself on the left file of the first platoon.

The guide having arrived at the distance of three paces from the line of battle, this platoon will be halted, as prescribed for the first; at the instant it halts its guide will spring on the line of battle, opposite to one of the three left files of his platoon, and will be assured in his position by the instructor.

The chief of the second platoon, seeing all its files in line, and its guide established on the direction, will command:

    *Right—*DRESS.

Having given this command, he will return to his place as a file-closer, passing around the left; the second platoon will dress up on the alignment of the first, and, when established, the captain will command:

    FRONT.

The movement ended, the instructor will command:

Guides—Posts.

At this command the two guides will return to their places in line of battle.

A column by platoon, left in front, will form on the left into line of battle, according to the same principles, and, by inverse means, applying to the second platoon what is prescribed for the first, and reciprocally. The chief of the second platoon having aligned it, from the point of *appui* (the left,) will retire to his place as a file-closer. The captain having halted the first platoon three paces behind the line of battle, will go to the same point to align this platoon, and then command: Front. At the command, *guides—posts,* given by the instructor, the captain will shift to his proper flank, and the guides take their places in the line of battle.

Formation of a company from two ranks into four, and reciprocally, at a halt, and in march.

172. The company being formed in two ranks, at a halt, and supposed to form part of a column right in front, when the instructor shall wish to form it into four ranks, he will command:

1. *In four ranks, form company.* 2. *Company left*—Face. 3. March (or *double quick*—March.)

At the second command, the left guide will remain faced to the front, the company will face to the left; the rear rank will gain the distance of one pace from the front rank by a side-step to the left and rear, and the men will form into four ranks as prescribed in the school of the soldier.

At the command *march,* the first file of four men will reface to the front without undoubling. All the other files of four will step off, and closing successively to about five inches of the preceding file, will halt, and immediately face to the front, the men remaining doubled.

The file-closers will take their new places in line of battle, at two paces in rear of the fourth rank.

The captain will superintend the movement.

173. The company being in four ranks, when the instructor shall wish to form it into two ranks, he will command:

1. *In two ranks, form company.* 2. *Company right*—Face. 3. March (or *double quick*—March.)

At the second command the left guide will stand fast, the company will face to the right.

At the command *march,* the right guide will step off and march in the prolongation of the front rank. The leading file of four men will step off at the same time, the other files standing fast; the second file will step off when there shall be between it and the first space sufficient to form it into two ranks. The following files will execute successively what has been prescribed for the second. As soon as the last file shall have its distance, the instructor will command:

1. *Company.* 2. Halt. 3. Front.

At the command *front,* the company will face to the front, and the files will undouble.

174. The company being formed in two ranks, and marching to the front, when the instructor shall wish to form it into four ranks, he will command:

1. *In four ranks, form company.* 2. *By the left, double files.* 3. March—(or *double quick*—March.)

At the command *march,* the left guide and the left file of the company will continue to march straight to the front; the company will make a half face to the left, the odd numbers placing themselves behind the even numbers. The even numbers of the rear rank will shorten their steps a little, to permit the odd numbers of the front rank to get between them and the even

numbers of that rank. The files thus formed of fours, except the left file,
will continue to march obliquely, lengthening their steps slightly, so as to
keep constantly abreast of the guide; each file will close successively on the
file next on its left, and when at the proper distance from that file, will face
to the front by a half face to the right, and take the touch of elbows to the
left.

175. The company being in march to the front in four ranks, when the instructor shall wish to form it into two ranks, he will command:

1. *In two ranks, form company.* 2. *By the right, undouble files.* 3. MARCH.
(or *double quick*—MARCH.)

At the command *march*, the left guide and the left file of the company will
continue to march straight to the front; the company will make a half face
to the right and march obliquely, lengthening the step a little, in order to
keep, as near as possible, abreast of the guide. As soon as the second file
from the left shall have gained to the right the interval necessary for the
left file to form into two ranks, the second file will face to the front by a
half face to the left and march straight forward; the left file will immediately form into two ranks, and take the touch of elbows to the left.
Each file will execute successively what has just been prescribed for the file
next to the left, and each will form into two ranks when the file next on its
right has obliqued the required distance and faced to the front.

If the company be supposed to make part of a column, left in front, these
different movements will be executed according to the same principles and by
inverse means, substituting the indicating *left* for *right*.

ARMY ORGANIZATION.

No. 8. The Captain on the right of the company, touching with the left elbow.
The first Sergeant, in the rear rank, touching with the left elbow, and covering
the captain. In the manœuvres he is denominated Covering Sergeant, or right
guide of the company.
The remaining officers and Sergeants are posted as file-closers, in the rank of
file-closers, two paces behind the rear rank.
The first Lieutenant, opposite the centre of the fourth section.
The second Lieutenant, opposite the centre of the first platoon.
The third Lieutenant, opposite the centre of the second platoon.
The second Sergeant, opposite the second file from the left of the company. In
the manœuvres he is called the left guide of the company.
The third Sergeant, opposite the second file from the right of the second platoon.
The fourth Sergeant, opposite the second file from the left of the first platoon.
The fifth Sergeant, opposite the second file from the right of the first platoon.
The Corporals are posted in the front rank, as directed in No. 7.

7. In the organization of infantry, the smallest number complete in itself, is the
Company, which varies in number from 50 to 100 rank and file.
A Captain, two or more Lieutenants, from four to six Sergeants, and as many
Corporals, are attached to every company. The Captain and Lieutenants are the
officers, the Sergeants and Corporals the non-commissioned officers of the company.
The Captain is responsible for the instruction, discipline, general efficiency, and
moral tone of the company.
The Lieutenants assist the Captain in the maintenance of discipline, and in the
instruction.
The company is divided into two equal parts, which are designated as the first
and second platoon, counting from the right, and each platoon is, in like manner,
divided into two sections.
The company is formed into two ranks in the following manner: the corporals
on the right and left of platoons, according to height; the tallest Corporal and the
tallest man from the first file on the right, the next two tallest men from the second
file, and so on to the last file, which is composed of the shortest Corporal and the
shortest man.
The odd and even files, numbered as one, two, in the company, from right to
left, form groups of four men, who, when they act as light troops, are designated
comrades in battle.

www.ingramcontent.com/pod-product-compliance
Lightning Source LLC
Chambersburg PA
CBHW031807090426
42739CB00008B/1198